IRONING THE LAND

IRONING
THE LAND

The Coming of the Railways to Ireland

KEVIN O'CONNOR

GILL & MACMILLAN

Gill & Macmillan Ltd

Goldenbridge

Dublin 8

with associated companies throughout the world

www.gillmacmillan.ie

© Kevin O'Connor 1999

0 7171 2747 8

Design and print origination by Identikit Design Consultants, Dublin

Printed by Butler & Tanner Ltd, Frome, Somerset

This book is typeset in 11pt on 15pt Berkeley Oldstyle.

A CIP catalogue record for this book is available from the
British Library.

1 3 5 4 2

Contents

Glossary

In railway parlance, the *permanent way* comprises the tracks, bolts and sleepers on which trains actually run. The term arose from railway construction, during which a temporary way was laid down on which construction wagons could be drawn. This was superseded by the finished or permanent way. The *gauge* is the width between the rails.

Abbreviations and footnotes test the patience of even the most dedicated of readers. I have tried to keep them to a minimum, consistent with readability, and have therefore not enumerated the many small companies who contributed to the Railway Age, or the hardy 'Junction' railways, founded to connect short distances between different main and branch lines. Some had brief life spans, while others were of surprising longevity before insolvency subsumed them into the wider picture.

For the purposes of this narrative, the main railways are:

D&BJR	Dublin & Belfast Junction Railway
D&DR	Dublin & Drogheda Railway
D&KR	Dublin & Kingstown Railway
D&SER	Dublin & South-Eastern Railway
DW&WR	Dublin, Wicklow & Wexford Railway
GNR	Great Northern Railway
GS&WR	Great Southern & Western Railway
MGWR	Midland Great Western Railway
UR	Ulster Railway

Dublin to Kingstown—
The First Commuter Railway

To understand the impact of the railways in the early nineteenth century, we have to remember how limited was human mobility at that time. The term 'public transport' had no meaningful currency, for the simple reason that there was none in the sense we understand today. Motor cars were fantasies of an inventor's drawing board. By the early 1800s, in spite of the progress of humankind in making historic treks for war or migration, people travelling a long distance went on foot, by water or on a rough cart drawn by a nag. A minority could afford to travel by horse-drawn carriage.

Canals and stagecoaches were the principal means of mass mobility, though 'mass' could mean twenty or so on a canal barge which progressed at three or four miles an hour. Of the various forms of horse transport, the larger stagecoaches lumbered along makeshift roads, often carrying excess weight which threatened stability. They were hauled at about six miles per hour by horses, which, due to the demanding loads, coupled with the state of the roads, required regular respite. Hence the need for staging posts, where fresh horses were put between the shafts and travellers were often so knocked about as to require more rest than the horses.

The better off travelled inside the coach with the female passengers, others might squeeze into the box seat next to the driver, while the rest clung to the top rails and to each other on rickety rides which spawned a wealth of complaining correspondence.

Roads in England, often following alignments laid down by the Romans, were the main arteries of movement, while in neighbouring Ireland a multiplicity of minor roads were a legacy of relief works from recurring famines since the previous

(Irish Railway Record Society)

Canal barges lumbered sedately at 3 or 4 mph. Horse-drawn stagecoaches moved at about twice that pace, with frequent stops to rest both horses and passengers, who sometimes needed it more after long bumpy rides over rough roads. An account from a traveller who went by coach from Strabane to Enniskillen in 1834:

(Ulster Folk & Transport Museum)

At first it drove on at a rapid rate, carrying about twenty-eight passengers, ten inside and eighteen on the outside, noisy and inebriated fellows . . . My feet had got numb with cold . . . When we had arrived within two yards of Seein Bridge, between Strabane and Newtownstewart, the lofty vehicle was thrown into the ditch, within two yards of a dangerous and steep bridge. If the vehicle had advanced about three yards further we would have been dashed to death.

Not an unusual account and part of what stimulated the evolution of railways for mass travel. The first carriages on rails were pulled by horses. When locomotives took to the rails, the precaution continued of having a rider on horseback travel ahead to check for obstruction of the line.

century. In the south of Ireland, Bianconi's 'long cars' could seat ten or so passengers on wooden benches which lined each side, exposed to the elements. Notoriously subject to hold-up and robbery, being confined to the wealthy, the more comfortable coaches plied the long haul on indifferent roads. However, the majority of people hardly moved outside their own parish. Not the least impact of the 'ironing of the land' would be the effect of mass mobility upon the social structures of the nineteenth century. The coming of the railways accelerated population movement, encouraged migration within countries and—coinciding with industrial production and the mass production of brick—helped form the urban base of population that most of us occupy today in towns and cities.

Nor was the impact of the railways confined within individual countries. In the formation of what were to become the great powers of the twentieth century, railways opened up vast territories in British colonies in Australia, Africa, Arabia, Asia and Canada. Railways helped consolidate the vast expanse of Russia into some kind of commonly connected, though unmanageable, political territory across time zones and climates. They also played a major part in welding the different states of North America into what was to become that powerhouse of the twentieth century, the United States.

All this mobility came about, in a century of rapid development, from the work of pioneers, the most famous of whom was George Stephenson. A Northumbrian of artisan stock, his experience on colliery lines gave him the opportunity to become locomotive superintendent of what is generally recognised as the world's first proper railway—the Stockton & Darlington Railway—which opened in 1825.

The early railways evolved from the use of tramways in the coal-mining industry. Pit ponies were used to haul heavy loads on wooden, and later iron, rails. These tramways were subsequently extended to take the coal to rivers, ports and canal basins for onward transit. Steam engines had been used to pump water from coal-mines since the early eighteenth century, and, in time, the technology of steam was applied to the colliery tramways to replace the ponies and horses which hauled the coal wagons. From these modest origins evolved the railway, which was to change the world in the nineteenth century.

The availability of copious amounts of cheap coal literally fuelled the boilers whose high pressure steam moved the pistons which turned the axles and the iron wheels—a circular momentum of coal, fire, steam, wheels—creating the iron horse driven by steam.

The railways marked the means by which the industrial age was made most visible on the landscape. Pit heads and factories, coal-mines and ports invested in

Railways evolved from the tramways needed to bring coal and miners to the surface. These were later extended to take the coal to the coast, to rivers or canals for shipment. On these first railways the coal trucks were drawn by horses. Later the use of steam became widespread, when coal was used to heat water to a constant 100°C to create a head of steam sufficient to drive the wheels. The steam locomotive had arrived and nothing would be the same again in the practice of moving people along a set of rails. (Mary Evans Picture Library)

rail connections as a means of getting goods to their destinations. They soon took over from canals and roads as the main arteries for commerce. The railways offered punctuality and comfort, increasing the traffic to music halls and large stores, to race meetings and religious convocations. A passion for railways took hold, spawned in the north of England, where the mines and factories powered industrial expansion.

The success of the S&DR opened the eyes of capitalists in other parts of England to the potential of the new mode of transport. Investors could see that profound changes were occurring in production and the transport of goods and people.

Railways, which began as a means of transporting coal to the ports, developed—quite unintentionally—into fashionable transport for people in the late nineteenth century, initially for the better off. Railways offered a new and convenient mobility to a previously locally-bound population.

The railways assisted the growth of education and literacy and thus were unwitting agents in the growth of democracy. Papers and magazines were transported on trains to outlying regions, informing people about the wider world, and fresh food was carried to the cities on the return journeys. The railways also led to advances in science and technology, from metallurgy to the electric telegraph.

All this development wrought irreversible change in the way people lived, coinciding with and becoming part of the expansion of the British empire. From then on, as the railways expanded in Britain and across the known world, they drove forward technology and imperialism. At the high point of the Industrial Revolution, Britain exported three-quarters of the world's locomotives and manufactured a million tons of rail for colonial economies, tracks along which travelled the administrators and armies of a burgeoning empire.

Conventional history has often overlooked the extent to which the railways were taken up by other powers to become the sinews of imperial expansion within the annexed territories. Imagine the impact of the iron road upon primitive transport systems in Asia and Africa—previously reliant upon barge and mule— and you glean something of the critical role of the railways in making manageable the colonial administrations of the nineteenth-century empires.

Because of its proximity to Britain, Ireland came early to the railways. Within months of the opening of the S&DR in 1825, a proposal was put before parliament to set up the first Irish railway. The first route to obtain parliamentary approval was between Waterford and Limerick. However, it would not be built for twenty years.

A potent body of promoters in Dublin took up the opportunity nearer the capital. Plans for this short stretch were resisted by owners of canals, by landlords

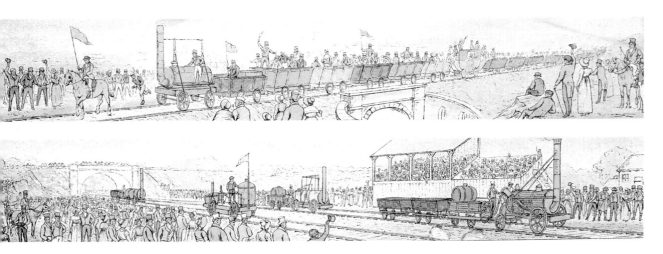

The opening of the Stockton & Darlington Railway in 1825 ushered in the railway age.
(Science Museum, London)

In the 1830s, three decades after the Act of Union brought Ireland into the United Kingdom, it was decided that the first railway would be between Dublin and the newly-named port of Kingstown. In spite of a docking pier stretching two miles into the bay, Dublin's historic port at the mouth of the Liffey was unable to offer berthing for the larger steamships, due to tidal silting. The Admiralty wanted to be able to move troops speedily from barracks to port, while the merchants of the 'Irish Sea Economic Area' needed to trade with Liverpool, Bristol and London using the fast railway movement of goods.

Kingstown was given royal imprimatur by King George IV (left) in a gala visit that ensured the commercial future of the port. (Mary Evans Picture Library)

of large country estates and by suppliers of carriage services between Dublin and Kingstown. Canal owners felt threatened by the enthusiasm for railways on the neighbouring island. Owners of extensive estates on the south side of Dublin, along the line of the intended route, were suspicious of any mode of transport which had the capacity to move large numbers of people, sensing the potential for disorder if volatile members of the 'lower orders' could be transported to the fringes of their estates.

Lobbyists against the railways usually had financial interests in the existing systems of transport. Meetings of interested parties were called to oppose the railway. During one such meeting, the idea that people would travel in great numbers by train to a seaside resort six miles outside of Dublin was dismissed by an MP as 'preposterous'—a comment which illustrates the static nature of most people's lives.

This combined opposition of vested interests defeated the first attempt to have parliament approve the proposed railway line from Dublin to Kingstown. But, with the growth of 'railway mania' in England, and the backing of companies there for a railway in Ireland, the opposition relented. Some became enthusiasts and promoted the railways as vigorously as they had opposed them, joining with the cartel of bankers in Dublin who were floating investment in a company they called the Dublin & Kingstown Railway.

Money and influence eased the passage of the Railway Bill, which noted its sponsors to be '. . . Gentlemen, Merchants, Traders, Freeholders and others of Dublin . . . subscribers to an intended Company to be called The Dublin and Kingstown Railway Company'. The Bill declared that the company would be formed 'under the authority of Parliament' and that the sum of £100,000 (equivalent to £5m) had been subscribed towards the opening of a 'certain and expeditious communication between the said city of Dublin and the Royal Harbour of Kingstown by affording an additional mode of conveyance for passengers and merchandise . . .'

The Irish promoters were well equipped to take risks. The main motivator was James Pim, who was a partner in a stockbroking firm in Dame Street, which was then the financial hub of Dublin. He lived in Monkstown, overlooking Kingstown harbour, and could see the potential of the proposed railway line for traffic between the port and the capital as his carriage took him to his office in Dublin along a road cluttered with all kinds of horse-drawn transport. In summer, the road was clouded like a desert storm with dust kicked up by wheels and hooves; in winter it could be a running stream of mud.

Dublin port had been built for sailing vessels, and, subject as it was to frequent silting, it could not offer shelter to the large iron steamships, whereas

Kingstown (Dún Laoghaire) was already expanding to provide berthage for these formidable vessels—further products of the Industrial Revolution. So Pim saw that Kingstown would be busy as a port for freight and passengers for the foreseeable future.

James Pim was a Quaker, a member of the Society of Friends—as were many of the promoters of the railways in England—which gave him an entrée into the privileged cartel. Pim was both an entrepreneur who believed that a proportion of his wealth should be used for the public good and a merchant adventurer with a desire to promote 'Progress', while having the means to do so. Of Pim's belief in the railway it was said: 'if he eats, drinks or sleeps he does it in connection with the Dublin & Kingstown Railway . . . the Railway seems to be chained to his mind—it moves when he moves and he moves where it moves'.

Pim made intensive studies of the railways in England, of passenger and freight returns. He received the active co-operation of the owners there and became a pivotal financier in what the historian Professor Joseph Lee has tagged the 'Irish Sea Economic Area', which consisted of merchants and bankers (mainly Quaker) who did business with each other out of the ports of Dublin, Liverpool, Cardiff, Bristol and London.

> These were compact family firms with, say, a father in Dublin and a son in Liverpool and another relative in Bristol. Their business was the financing of trade through the Irish and British ports, which by the 1820s were carrying an increasing amount of sea-traffic between the two islands because of the amount of goods being produced by the industrial revolution.

Ireland, with a population of about six million, provided a large market for goods produced in Britain and the colonies, as well as providing a constant supply of soldiery. Irish horses and agricultural produce were also in demand in Britain. Clearly, any improved system of transport which would make more efficient the 'expeditious delivery of goods and people' from the port to Dublin was likely to gain custom.

From connections which the D&KR directors had in Britain they were able to get assistance for their adventurous scheme—from those involved in both the promotion and generation of the lines already in business across the Irish Sea. Amongst these was the Irish-born engineer Charles Vignoles, whose appointment was insisted on by the Board of Works to safeguard their prospective investment of £75,000 in the scheme—half the cost. Another engineer, Thomas Bergin, was appointed secretary, overseeing the correspondence with the Board of Works. The conditions of the loan were strict, requiring repayment of interest after a year and

*Samuel Brocas'
1820 view of
Burgh Quay, the
Corn Exchange
and the Custom
House. Prior to
the railway age
Dublin was
overwhelmingly
a maritime city,
its connections
with England
more constant
than those with
many parts of
its Irish
hinterland.
(National
Library of
Ireland)*

*William Dargan. The
D&KR was built by the
contractor William Dargan.
A farmer's son from Carlow,
he displayed an early gift
for mathematics. His
apprenticeship in England
to Telford, who made him
responsible for the work on
stretches of the road from
London to Holyhead,
consolidated his skills in
road making and
management of the
construction workers.
Telford recommended
Dargan to the promoters of
the D&KR and helped him
secure the contract.
(Iarnród Éireann)*

making the personal wealth of the promoters, and their heirs, subject to forfeit in the event of bankruptcy.

In contrast to some of the protracted parliamentary debates which had characterised the granting of some railways in England, the comparatively short distance of the Dublin–Kingstown line and the care taken in preparing land surveys and projections of traffic helped expedite the D&KR passage through parliament.

The War Department noted that it would be possible to move troops speedily through the port of Kingstown, feeling that, if Irish life continued to be punctuated by periodic armed rebellions—the most severe, in 1798, was still within living memory—or if the country was invaded by the French as a prelude to an attack on England, then rail transport should be an active consideration for those planning military response.

With all these forces dictating the need for a railway somewhere on the island, probably near the capital, the determining factor for its location was economic. James Pim and the merchant interests who made up the 'Irish Sea Economic Area' were the effective creators of the railway, riding on a convergence of political and military interests. The gauge chosen for the new line was 4 ft 8½ inches, which was widely used in Britain.

The company was charged with getting the railways built to specific standards of safety and construction. In the founding of the D&KR, James Pim and James Perry, who had experience of canal investment, administered the finances and 'politics', and Charles Vignoles oversaw the engineering. Thomas Bergin was secretary and general manager and William Dargan the contractor.

Dargan, the son 'of a respectable tenant farmer' in rural Carlow, displayed an early aptitude for mathematics and had taken an apprenticeship as a surveyor. Developing into a naturally gifted builder, he was recommended by his local MP Henry Brooke Parnell—who later became Secretary of State for War in the British cabinet—to the Scottish-born contractor Telford, who built the road from London to the port of Holyhead, then one of the great feats of road making.

In his home constituency in Ireland, Parnell had often complained to the young Dargan about the state of the roads between the Irish midlands and Dublin. From a dawn start in Carlow, it took about twelve hours to travel the 80 meandering miles to Dublin by stagecoach before embarking upon a sea journey and then a further day's travel to parliament in London. The journey was considerably reduced by 'Telford's road', as the stretch from Holyhead to London was known.

By the time he reached his thirties Dargan was in charge of major stretches of road and canal making, where he came into contact with the navvies. He appreciated the skills of these rough gangs of migrant labourers and learned to get the best out of them by treating them decently. In England in the 1820s, agricultural labourers were coming off the land and finding employment in the building of roads and railways. Most were treated literally as 'lumpen labour', to be hired or fired at will. (The 'lump' has continued as a term in the construction industry, meaning casual labour.)

Dargan's experience proved invaluable when his tender to build the Dublin to Kingstown railway was accepted. While his expertise had evolved from canal and road building, some of the same skills applied in laying down a rail route— excavating and making cuttings, shaping embankments and building bridges to carry the railway over roads, culverts and gulleys.

The D&KR budget comprised Dargan's detailed costing of labour and equipment and banker Pim's allowances for land purchase, with another £20,000 for unforeseen contingencies (equivalent to £1m). The directors' projections of passenger numbers were based on analysis of the existing traffic between Dublin and Kingstown, which showed that, if sufficient switched to rail usage, the railway would be a commercial success. Their survey counted 70,000 journeys a month using all modes of transport. Of these, 5,000 were in private carriages, 19,000 in private jaunting cars, over 6,000 by 'saddle horse' and 24,000 in 'public cars', the remainder being made up of trade carts, gigs and jingles and many other means of horse transport.

One can easily glean from these figures the prevailing reliance on the horse, from well-bred carriage horses down to the cobs of coster-mongers. Averaging those census figures to 2,300 journeys a day between Dublin and Kingstown, the promoters were confident in the ability of the new railroad to take enough of that traffic to make their railway pay.

From the beginning the intention was to provide a full daily service between Dublin and Kingstown, seven return journeys from morning until evening, with carriages for 300 passengers and enough stops to cater for the districts along the way. The D&KR confidently expected that the novelty of rail travel, and the proximity of the port and its seasonal attractions, would in time make for profitable usage.

They calculated a revenue of about £30,000 over a year, against operating costs of £10,000. Moreover, the newly-named port of Kingstown, attracting cross-channel passenger, freight and mail business, was expanding into a holiday resort for well-off Dubliners. Responding to new objections from residents who feared the effects of the masses travelling, the promoters asserted that the railway could only enhance the port and become an agent of its expansion, generating even more commerce. One of their notices has an oddly modern ring:

A wealthy and eccentric landowner, Baron Cloncurry lived at Maretimo House near Blackrock (left). Refusing permission for the railway to traverse the foreshore of his farming land, he extorted payment of the equivalent of £150,000 in today's money. The railway company was required to build a bridge over the line 'in the best Italianate style' to allow Cloncurry to access a bathing hut, which the company also had to build, modelled on a Greek 'pleasure-dome for men'.

DART travellers pass by both relics, though most are oblivious as to how these architectural oddities came to decorate their commuter line. The original route was carved out by William Dargan in 1836. (National Library of Ireland)

These two views of the fine Italianate bridge across Lord Cloncurry's land, built in the early, heroic days of the D&KR, demonstrate some of the difficulties that Dargan faced and the elegance and creativity with which he overcame them. Extreme left is the Greek-style bathing dome which the railway company built in compensation. (Science Museum, London)

The railway with its trains of carriages in rapid motion, will form a novel and not uninteresting foreground . . . Kingstown will become a resort to which all classes will be attracted by the opportunity for the enjoyment of healthy exercise amidst a pure atmosphere and romantic surroundings.

The line would run from near Trinity College, from a new terminus which was to be built behind the houses at Westland Row. It would follow a route across the Grand Canal and out along the coast, hugging the extremity of the land and occasionally crossing water on stoutly-built embankments. The foundations of these embankments were to be of hard-core, dressed with granite, and would be laid on packed sand and rock, protected by a buttressing of granite and limestone, sufficient to resist tidal sea forces.

Stations would be at key residential areas along the way, and the train would ply its coastal route over roads and rivers to deliver its passengers to a station at Kingstown, near the harbour. As published in notices and commented upon in the Dublin broadsheets, the public was entranced by the prospect of a railway, which only those who had been to England had experienced. But there was considerable work still to do, even as the plans of the 1830s gained credence with 'a multitudinous public, hungry for sensation'.

Hearings before a Land Jury to arbitrate on compensation to landowners over whose property the line would run became demanding of time and money. By the curve along the sea at Blackrock, two landowners whose estates ran to the foreshore escalated their prices. Baron Cloncurry and a clergyman, the Reverend Lees, made demands which drew heavily on the company finances. Cloncurry, a wealthy and eccentric peer who had been jailed for his anti-government activities on behalf of Irish nationalists, maintained that the new line would destroy the privacy of his bathing area and that the railway running by his estate would expose him to the gaze of the populace on his walk from home to sea. The company considered the alternative of tunnelling underneath the 'ransom' lands to keep the railway out of his view—and the passengers from looking into the grounds of his estate—but it would have involved even greater costs and delays, as well as the dangers which tunnelling invariably involved.

After much haggling, Baron Cloncurry agreed to let the railway build on the foreshore, on payment of £3,000 (equivalent to £150,000), with the added condition that the company would provide a bridge across the line by which he could, with his dogs, access his private bathing area—the bridge to be built 'in the best Italianate style'. The company would also build a granite bathing hut by the sea, modelled on a Greek 'pleasure-dome for men'. The other objector, Reverend

Lees, settled for the exorbitant sum of £7,500 (equivalent to £375,000). The protracted negotiations cost Dargan two months of headway, while the compensation was a heavy drain on capital.

With those obstacles behind him, Dargan continued with clearing, soil testing and drainage. By the measure of the time it was a formidable undertaking, which fired the curiosity of Dubliners who came in droves to observe the initial earthworks, the array of labouring skills being used and the sheer scale of what was promised. They got value for their sightseeing. William Dargan had recruited a workforce of 1,000 labourers to forge the route along the coast. The labourers first set about the headlands, like squads of army sappers, demolishing the juttings along the coastal way and conserving the spoil for later use in levelling. There was no shortage of male muscle, deployed to 'take down nature's inheritance'.

Census figures calculated that there were about two million unemployed men on the island, practically all of whom were experienced in some kind of farm work but not in urban construction work. The railway began with demolition, excavation and conservation of soil and rock. Gangs of navvies had been recruited from the canal and railway construction industry in England and these skilled and hardened workers were deployed simultaneously to different parts of the line. It took a year on the railway to make a labourer into a navvy who could work a full day shifting 'muck', as the heavy clay was called. Many were extended families of workmen from different parts of Ireland and some were from Liverpool and Scotland. They were paid a piece-work rate, which was essentially earning according to the amount of muck they could shift, the quantity being assessed by overseers who measured the loads in wheelbarrows.

The weaponry of this army of 1,000 navvies were pickaxes to break the ground and shovels to take out the earth and stones; rudimentary block-and-tackle methods of putting the loads into wheelbarrows; horse-carts to truck the stuff away—the entire excavation driven by sheer muscle and grit. According to Terry Coleman, historian of the railway navvies in England, nothing like this scale of physical effort would have been recorded since the building of the pyramids in Egypt or the medieval cathedrals in Europe, enterprises unique to their times which absorbed many generations of continuous labour.

In Ireland in 1833, the first railway made a similar impact, with the men who dug the way becoming an élite of the proletariat around whom legend quickly formed. They were capable of extraordinary feats. An experienced navvy could, in a 12-hour day, by constant use of pick and shovel, dig out and sling over his shoulder piles of heavy, clinging clay amounting to about 20 tons. He could also put away two pounds of beef per day and replenish his sweat with a dozen quarts of beer. They did not live long: it was rare to meet an old navvy. The Donegal-born writer Patrick Magill worked among the migrant Irish navvies:

> How dies the navvie man—the bold navvie man?
> Safe in the ditch with toes turned up—thus dies the navvie man.

A clergyman, the Reverend St George Sargent, recalled his parsonage at the Mendicity Institute in Dublin:

> I think they are the most neglected and spiritually destitute people I ever met . . . ignorant of Bible religion and gospel truth, infected with infidelity and very often with revolutionary principles.

It was a harsh judgement upon a workforce which was living primitively, divided into clannish groupings and earning a subsistence wage that no amount of Bible reading could transform into sustenance. The 'revolutionary principles' took fire in June of 1833, when gathering resentment at the wages led to agitation. Meetings and stoppages were called and, as one newspaper described it:

> The infatuated workmen at Seapoint objected to work unless paid ten shillings per week instead of nine. One man called together several of the workmen and whistling 'St Patrick's Day' and 'The Boyne Water' led them through masses of labourers on the shore, encouraging them not to work unless they received higher salaries.

The rioting that ensued provoked police retaliation and the entire work ground to a stop until Dargan intervened with an offer of piece-work—payment according to work done—an offer which was made after the jailing of the leaders of the unrest. He persuaded Pim and Bergin to concede improved conditions and increases in pay, based on the amounts of 'muck' excavated.

Navvies followed the work; few had settled wives with them, but they formed makeshift family groupings with the women who joined them in the encampments and shanty dwellings which grew up around the line of the railway. In England they had been called 'banditi', because of their swarthy appearance from the constant grime in which they worked and because of their rapacious reputation. In Dublin, they seem to have caused less offence, as they camped by Ringsend and City Quay among the seafaring communities.

As a parliamentary inquiry was later to be told:

> They are brought hastily together in large bodies; no time is given for that gradual growth of accommodation which would naturally accommodate the gradual growth of numbers. They are exposed to great risks of life and limb . . . and many inducements to be thoughtless, thriftless and improvident.

Alan Fearnley

Navvies were products of the industrial age, hired to make canals and railways. The primitive equipment used by the early navvies included picks, shovels and cart-horses, and elaborate wooden shuttering for excavation work. Later they had the benefit of steam-shovels (left).

It was rare to find a navvy aged fifty; most succumbed to accident and ill health in their forties. At their most prolific as journeyman builders, they were an élite of the proletariat: objects of fear and fascination in the districts to which they journeyed to make the railway.

The 'inducements to be thriftless and improvident' were, in fact, the conditions demanded of their nomadic work. They needed to be mobile, rough and ready, and, above all, willing. They were compared to a battle-hardened army. Spending what they earned, having the tag 'pioneers', which was an army name for tunnellers in sieges, the higher paid were in receipt of wages amounting to the magical 'half a quid' (ten shillings) a week, considerably more than most could earn by farm labouring where a shilling a day was a rare wage. The navvies earned a reputation as hard grafters and fighters. A country which was mainly agricultural had seen nothing like this urbanised army wielding pick and shovel. In a few months, from Westland Row to Ringsend, the accumulating earthworks of their endeavours starkly changed the landscape along the line of the proposed railway.

It is difficult, nearly 170 years after it was first proposed, to convey just how audacious a venture was the promotion of Ireland's first railway—to link the city of Dublin with the developing port of Kingstown. Think of it in terms of a private company promoting space travel in the early 1960s, a few years after the first satellites had been launched.

Transport in Ireland changed forever in October 1834 when the locomotives *Vauxhall* and *Hibernia* were shipped from the Mersey to the Liffey. They were pulled through the dockside streets to Westland Row on temporary rails, followed by large crowds who watched as teams of men levered and lifted the steam-engines onto the newly-built line. With a celebratory lighting of its fire box (with coke), *Vauxhall* travelled with much fanfare to a point near Blackrock, and five days later steamed the full journey to Kingstown.

The intention was to have the line fully operational by the end of the year, but that target was threatened when storm flooding brought down the culvert bridge at Landsdowne. Protracted repairs on other landslides further threatened to delay the completion date. However, Dargan's determination to have the route operational by the end of 1834 finally paid off. On 17 December 1834 at 9.30 a.m., running 30 minutes late, the locomotive *Hibernia*, built in Manchester, leading a train of carriages carrying a 'fashionable concourse of persons'— representing most of Dublin's ruling class—travelled the full stretch down to Kingstown harbour, cheered along by a 'gathering of the citizenry' who lined both sides of the embankments.

As was recorded in the *Dublin Evening Post* of Thursday 18 December 1834:

This splendid work was yesterday opened to the public for the regular transmission of passengers to and from Kingstown, and the immediate stage at the Black-rock. Notwithstanding the early hour at which the first train started, half-past nine

*December 1834.
The opening of the
D&KR was a sensation.
Here the first train crosses
Cumberland Street Bridge,
southbound to Kingstown.
(National Library
of Ireland)*

*Steaming into history.
An early view of the
D&KR, southbound at
Merrion, showing first-,
second-, third- and
fourth-class (uncovered)
carriages, with Howth in
the background.
The carriages are pulled
by the locomotive
Hibernia. (National
Library of Ireland)*

*An early lithograph of
the D&KR, looking
north from Blackrock
at the approaching
train. This fine view
was made in 1834, the
year the service began,
and gives a particularly
good impression of the
embankment which
Dargan built across
Merrion Strand, thus
creating Booterstown
Marsh (on the left).
(Science Museum,
London)*

o'clock, the carriages were filled by a very fashionable concourse of persons, and the greatest eagerness was manifested to witness the first operations of the work. Up to a quarter past five the line of road from Merrion to Salthill was thronged with spectators, who loudly cheered each train that passed them. The average rate at which the trip was performed yesterday was nineteen minutes and a half, including a delay of about two minutes at the Rock, where passengers were taken up.— Much confusion was occasioned at starting by the want of proper arrangement, but this inconvenience will be very easily obviated. The utmost precautions were, however, taken to prevent the possibility of accident, by stationing men at proper intervals along the road, and the trains at starting were propelled slowly for a short distance for the same object. Although there could not have been less than from three to four thousand persons upon the railway during the day, we are happy to state that these very necessary precautions were attended with the desired effect.

The Times of Monday 22 December 1834 saw it as a notable 'Irish' event.

Ireland   *(From our own correspondent.)*

Dublin, Dec 17.

This day our Kingstown Railroad opened, under very favourable auspices. Crowds thronged the offices at West-land-row, and every hour a full train of carriages started "at high pressure." Every one engaged in the works seems in excellent spirits at the satisfactory state of the road, engines, carriages, &c. All the machinery works well as yet, except in one particular: the springs are not sufficiently elastic to prevent sudden shocks when the carriages stop. Three or four gentlemen had one occasion to-day their heads knocked against each other and the carriage doors, and severe contusions were the consequence. A county of Kildare gentleman's head was laid open. The majority had, however, hard Irish heads, and did not mind a few knocks. The directors have prepared a splendid entertainment at Kingstown for their friends and the subscribers to the undertaking. The weather is delightful for December, and a few broken heads does not throw much damp on a scene of Irish amusement, where everything else goes well.

With the Irish Sea on one side and rising land on the other, the *Hibernia's* journey was the public opening of the island's first fare-paying railway. According to some railway historians it also became the world's first commuter run, as in time a residential population settled along its route, using the line to travel in and out of Dublin. It was the first time that people of differing professions and status had travelled within collective sight of each other, a 'close consanguinity' that the novelist Charles Lever found amusing:

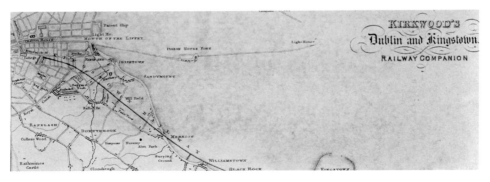

'Land ahoy!' The first locomotive, Hibernia. Nine British companies were invited to bid for the supply of the engines, whose specifications required that 'all must be perfect counterparts of each other, so that every individual bolt, screw, spring, connecting rod, in short every part of one engine may equally fit any of the other'. Two manufacturers were selected, from Liverpool and Manchester, whose specimen engines, Vauxhall and Hibernia, were shipped to Dublin and pulled through the streets by teams of workmen, followed by excited crowds who watched the engines being levered up onto the railway tracks. (Science Museum, London)

An early panorama and map of the D&KR. A train is northbound along the embankment at Merrion—still a novelty and a thing of wonder to passers-by. The embankment on which it is travelling is clearly shown at the bottom of the map. (National Library of Ireland)

The 8.30 a.m. is filled with attorneys; the ways of Providence are inscrutable; it arrives safely in Dublin. With the 9.00 train come fresh jovial looking fellows with bushy whiskers and geraniums in buttonholes. They are traders. 9.30 is the housekeepers train. 10.00 the barristers—fierce faces look out at the weather . . . 11 o'clock, the men of wit and pleasure.

The D&KR became the unifying corridor of transport between the suburbs and the capital. For an era which seems so dim and distant, there were flashes of gaiety and modernity, with the outside of some carriages painted in gaudy colours, while the first-class carriages were painted Prussian blue, the universal colour of the ruling class on state occasions.

The D&KR became a model railway, in that it was built to exacting standards of construction and was efficiently run, with customer needs paramount, claiming a million passenger journeys in its first year. The *Vauxhall* and *Hibernia* started at opposite ends of the double-tracked line. They ran from early morning until late evening, leaving passengers within walking distance of their homes. They consistently carried full complements of 300 passengers, travelling at an average speed of over 20 mph.

Over 160 years on, it is essentially the same route travelled by the DART (Dublin Area Rapid Transit), which carries upwards of 80,000 commuters to and from the capital every day; about half that number travel on the original route of the D&KR.

As predicted by Pim and his fellow directors, the coming of the railway increased the amount of people travelling in and out of Kingstown. The company met operating targets, built more stations, and carried the overnight letters and parcels from the 'mail packet' from England. It kept its rolling stock in good order, replenished carriages and locomotives and, in time, had the satisfaction of refusing to grant the Reverend Lee a station convenient to his residence, even though—as a late convert to the railway—he offered to donate the site.

The D&KR made handsome profits, from which was repaid the interest and capital, half of which had been advanced by the Board of Works. The shareholders of the other half of the capital—and their heirs—were in beneficial receipt of regular 10 per cent dividends for many years.

For William Dargan, who was to become a 'builder extraordinaire' in an era of pioneering reputations and who would go on to build many hundreds of miles of railways throughout Ireland, the completion of the D&KR taught him many new lessons and confirmed old ones in the 'true art of road-making' on a stretch of railway line that today is still accessible for those who wish to see what went into making a nineteenth-century railroad—the first on the island.

These two illustrations, made almost 50 years apart, show the development of the
system in the Victorian age. Both views are from the Martello tower bridge at
Seapoint. The photograph below, taken late in the nineteenth century, shows the
dramatic building development in the wake of the railway.
(National Library of Ireland)

The Great Northern Railway—
Dublin to Belfast

A lthough Dublin was the acknowledged political capital of Ireland since before the Act of Union of 1801, Belfast had a strong, separate sense of itself as the industrial capital. Different in commercial texture and social make-up, with an urban base of textile manufacturing and vigorous trade through an expanding port, the burghers of Belfast embraced the values and rewards of the Industrial Revolution more zealously than Dublin. At the time of the 1841 census, when the railways were taking shape in the north and south of the island, Belfast had about a third of Dublin's population (Belfast 70,447, Dublin 232,726). By the 1891 census, the population of Belfast had exceeded that of the capital (Belfast 276,114, Dublin 269,716).

As the railways gained ground in Britain, the factory owners of Belfast, whose considerable fortunes had been made in the mass production of textiles using steam technology, formed a business association and lobbied to have a railway. Parliamentary debates and submissions followed and, when the Bill went for royal assent, the published list of the promoters included several owners of the larger linen mills. A prime promoter was Andrew Mulholland, whose use of industrial technology had vastly increased the spinning of yarn from flax and expanded the mills in Belfast.

Mulholland, Wallace, Greer, Montgomery, Gunning and MacNamara were among the names which undertook to fund 'The Ulster Railway Company', which was authorised by parliament to make:

A railway from the town of Belfast to the city of Armagh in the Province of Ulster . . . which will prove of great public advantage, by the opening of an additional,

Waiting and waiting . . . The terminals of the Dublin–Belfast link lay at Amiens Street station,
Dublin, and Great Victoria Street station, Belfast. (Ulster Museum)

*cheap, certain and expeditious communication between the port of Belfast and the
city of Armagh . . . and with several intermediate towns and places.*

These 'intermediate' towns would include Lisburn, Lurgan and Portadown.

As was now standard, the Bill pertinently noted that the investors would be
willing 'at their own Costs and Charges to carry into execution the said
Undertaking'. In 1836, the government was all too conscious of the number of
debtors that littered the courts in the aftermath of unfinished lines at the height
of the Railway Mania. Ten years of building enthusiasm had incurred casualties in
the bankruptcy courts, as well as convictions against some developers.

With results from hole boring and soil testing completed during 1836 (two
years after the opening of the Dublin & Kingstown Railway), preliminary surveying
and digging began in early 1837. The stated objective of the promoters of the UR
was to bring the population of the Lagan Valley within the railway compass, thereby
providing speedier access for the workers to the textile mills. Just as the first railway
in Britain had developed out of the need to move coal from mines to cities and
ports, the project was driven by industrial and commercial considerations.

Construction work progressed from early 1837. As with all physical work at
the time, it was heavy, skilled and took little account of the welfare of the men and
horses. Injuries and loss of limbs seem to have provoked few inquiries as the line
proceeded, with the fervour of the age and against the odds. Winter saw the
horses and navvies knee-deep in swamp on the stretches outside of Belfast known
as the Bog Meadows, giving rise to many cases of pneumonia and pleurisy. North
of Dunmurry, the navvies encountered stretches of heavy, clinging clay which the
unusually wet weather turned into a quagmire.

By the following summer, conditions were not much better. Having left the
bog behind, the navvies were now encountering earth which was hard to dig with
shovel and pickaxe, while the insanitary living conditions added diarrhoea and
dysentery to their hardships. The gangers, or foremen, rode up and down the line
on horseback upbraiding the navvies, by whose work they would earn profits but
for whose welfare they were not responsible. As frequent testimony of that time
shows, when a man fell on hard times or his health broke there was little help for
him beyond reliance on his own kind for rudimentary medicine and a share of
their earnings until—as the case may be—he recovered or died.

To understand their condition one has to remember that this was the age of
inequality as much as of industrial revolution. In the British Isles of the mid-
1800s, public hangings or deportation were in force for theft. The labouring
classes upon whose muscle the industrial prosperity depended were called the

Columns and arches.
Construction of the Keady
Viaduct in County Armagh.
(Ulster Museum)

This fine Egyptian arch
carried the railway at
Bessbrook, County Armagh.
(Public Record Office of
Northern Ireland)

'lower orders' and were confined to slum habitation, without rights to education. Navvies tramped from job to job, making what money they could and frequently falling foul of foremen and gangers. Most navvies were broken in health by forty, dead by fifty.

And yet, and yet . . . the pictures that survive from a somewhat later time show little of that privation. Instead, we have the overseers: stern men in waistcoats, others in leggings and moleskins, posing in portraits of sculpted pride. They stand alongside the stonemasons who cut the blocks for bridges and embankments, the chippies who made the wooden shuttering to keep out water, the shovellers who dug the muck—all pictured in harmony by the wooden scaffoldings upon which they would construct bridges and viaducts with the panache of Roman field commanders.

Over all these were the 'subbies' (sub-contractors), who in turn had been granted specific stretches of work to complete at a set price. Their profit came from the difference between the price agreed with the contractor and what they paid their men. Many of the subbies also operated the 'truck system', where a truck containing picks and shovels, moleskins and boots and sometimes alcohol would ply the labouring lines. The navvies were sold a pickaxe and shovel (which they had to supply in order to work) on credit against their wages, which in effect meant that many received little hard cash at the end of a month. (Most were paid monthly.) As a result there were frequent arguments about being left short by the subbies. The navvie usually came off worse, as he was fired for complaining. Navvies would often simply leave a job in disgust and tramp off to another part of the line, hoping to find a less oppressive subbie and more congenial conditions.

Out of these primitive conditions were laid the first stretches of railway out of Belfast. Ulster's varied landscape was being traversed by the railroad, literally up hill and down dale, across valleys that had not been bridged before, skirting drumlin country and laying foundations in gorse fields, to link trade, commerce and farming in the most populated province in Ireland.

Although it was far from the commercial intentions of the proprietors, the railway was pulling together disparate cultures, linking town and country. In the wider context, the north-east of the island was being subjected to the iron will of the railway. Nothing would ever be the same again, not only in the landscape, but in terms of the labour made available to the industrial hinterland of Belfast. In Ulster the railway consolidated a manufacturing economy that was ahead of anywhere else on the island.

George Stephenson was a consultant engineer to UR, which was more closely modelled on the original railway in England. His was a name that looked good on the prospectus, although he spent no more than a few days in Ulster at the end of October and beginning of November in 1836. The redoubtable William Dargan, with the achievement of the D&KR under his belt, was the contractor for most of the works. By now a legend among the workers, Dargan monitored the work in his personal coach, which was fitted out as a travelling head office with living quarters.

He appears to have had the gift of dealing fairly with a large and disparate workforce, made up of many potentially disruptive elements. The notable absence of damaging strikes or sabotage may be ascribed to Dargan's genuine fellow-feeling for his employees, whose numbers at times exceeded 3,000 men. According to the published correspondence, he adroitly avoided conflict by paying demands out of his own personal funds when workers were faced with stoppages because of mass outbreaks of fever. Similarly, he 'topped-up' basic wages with payment for piece-work which related earnings to the advance of the line.

As the UR got under way, nomadic gangs were employed for long stretches towards Lisburn and Portadown, requiring them to make temporary homes of any available sheds and outhouses. In pursuit of their railway dream, many of them had become itinerant workers, having left work on farms for the railway, trading up their basic agricultural skills to the railway construction. To move rank from labourer to navvy took about a year and required stamina with pick and shovel over a long day, 'come rain, come shine'. Becoming a navvy required graft and craft—in running heavy loads up inclined planks and turning aside at the top to let the load disgorge by its own momentum into the far side of the pile, without going in after it.

Most of all, the railway navvies required quantities of sheer grit to shift the muck: tons and tons of it, from what must have appeared a bottomless pit of excavation. Living rough in 'families' of loose blood-line, hunkering down at night in strange townlands, it is hardly surprising that their coming was recorded with fascination by local scribes, or that their departure was observed with relief.

'Living in a state of utter barbarism' was how one account described the hovels of turf and mud, while another noted:

> There was no separation between the beds; in one slept a man and his wife and one or two children, in another a couple of young men, in a third bed in the same hut another man and his wife and family.

Such conditions were not unusual in the cities of the mid-nineteenth century as people flocked from the countryside, which was often subject to localised famines and plagues. But with the navvies reversing the migration by moving into the countryside, there was simply insufficient accommodation.

The Ballyards Viaduct under construction on 23 December 1904. 'Building with the panache of Roman field-commanders', railway construction continued throughout the nineteenth century and into the twentieth.

The railway station at Portadown, on the Dublin to Belfast line, photographed in the late nineteenth century. By 1876 the three companies that had built the Dublin to Belfast route had amalgamated to form the Great Northern Railway. This station, Portadown's third up to that time, was built by the Ulster Railway and opened in July 1863. It remained in use until 1970 when it was replaced by the much more basic station still in use today. The much-loved GNR survived until 1958. (National Library of Ireland)

Inns and hotels were for the well-off. The navvies worked seven days a week and were an uncomfortable intrusion on most rural communities, whereas the engineer and surveyor were regarded as the 'inventors' of the railway. Photographs of the time reveal engineers 'in suits', as befitted men who were potent in a pecking-order which ascribed a high status to 'engineer', the man who put order upon massive quantities of iron and steel.

Within two years of the first diggings, the line was ready for use between Belfast and Lisburn, a distance of seven and a half miles. The difficult terrain, bad weather and accidents accounted for the delay. Advertisements promoted round-trips to Lisburn at a cost of a shilling for a first-class carriage and sixpence for a second-class seat.

At first, travel was confined to first and second class, fares being beyond most labourers' means. In time, however, the class whose labour had made possible the enterprise was catered for: the UR introduced third-class travel in County Antrim in 1841. Some years on, the 'labouring classes' would prove to be the mainstay of the railway: they were provided with standing space in open goods wagons and, later again, with bench seats and reduced fares.

While the northerners were engaged in pushing on towards Armagh (via Lisburn and Portadown), in Dublin some of those who had successfully delivered the first railway on the island planned to extend another line as far as Drogheda. Previously, there had been plans to run a direct line from Dublin to Belfast, but no agreement was forthcoming from the merchants of the north, who wanted Armagh to be a terminus. Because Armagh was inland and not favoured by the Dublin entrepreneurs, they lobbied for a Bill to promote a line straight up the coast. The first stage would extend as far as Drogheda. The investors formed the Dublin & Drogheda Railway Company.

Alarmed by the prospect of competition and the perceived waste of a second line along the same route, UR asked the southern investors to move more inland. An Irish Railway Commission which reported in 1838 recommended the inland route. Work was then halted on the initial stretch of the coastal Dublin to Drogheda line, which had progressed about two miles north of Dublin.

The debate over an inland or a coastal link delayed the development of the project. For revenue reasons, the UR wanted Dublin traffic to run along their line from Armagh. The UR's commercial concerns were amplified by doubts as to whether the hills between Dundalk and Newry could be surmounted by a railway at this time: but there were genuine engineering concerns about the gradients north of Dundalk. This delay allowed the notional coastal link between Dublin and Belfast to be revived, though by this time—1840—the UR was well advanced towards Portadown, thereby keeping to a key stretch of the original route from Belfast.

When the work resumed, the D&DR company gave the renewed contract to William Dargan, who had overcome many obstacles to complete the Dublin to Kingstown line, then the pioneering example of a finished, durable railway. Dargan's experience with the seaward laying of the D&KR line had taught him costly lessons about erosion of foundations. Heading for Drogheda, he avoided sinking embankments at the seafront at Clontarf, going inland for a while, then emerging again to a coastal sweep at Malahide, heading northwards over a bridge across the estuary.

By the turn of the year of 1842, even as the line out of Belfast was reaching the outskirts of Portadown, in the south there were trial runs out of Amiens Street as far as Skerries. A celebratory run to Drogheda carried the Lord Lieutenant of Ireland and his retinue of nobility among 540 passengers in what was clearly a journey of political significance.

Daniel O'Connell was also a vigorous proponent of railways, across many fronts: railways were progressive, they provided employment and traffic for commerce and export. But he was also a representative of Catholic interests in an overwhelmingly Protestant parliament, a leader of the dispossessed whose recent activities the government chose to see as 'inciting' armed rebellions. In the context of the railway, he helped outmanoeuvre the northern desire to turn the Dublin line inland to meet the UR's terminus at Armagh.

Days after the Lord Lieutenant's triumphal journey along the railroad, O'Connell was given a similar honour, including a military band. It had been deemed prudent not to have him accompany the Lord Lieutenant, who was preparing a charge of seditious conspiracy against O'Connell. Hence he was honoured with his own separate journey to see some of the fruits of his parliamentary labours, as expressed in the rail route to Drogheda.

While O'Connell believed in the railways as a mark of progress and had defended them against criticism, the fact was that the development of railways required capital, and the need to recover a return on the investment meant that, in the early years, rail travel was expensive. Other than to provide labour, the masses were largely excluded from the railway enthusiasm. In addition, there now arose the calamity of the Great Famine. Some of O'Connell's rural supporters even held that the smoke from the railways was poisoning the land, killing off crops and infecting cattle. The failure of the potato crop in 1845 alarmed thousands of rural smallholders whose circumstances were far removed from those embarking on

A posed portrait of Daniel O'Connell. (National Library of Ireland)

Engineer Sir John MacNeill.

Larne Viaduct around the turn of the century. (Public Record Office of Northern Ireland)

train journeys from Dublin to Malahide, celebrated by brass bands and military salutes from shore batteries.

By the spring of 1844, the D&DR was fully operational, the grand opening marked by a banquet 'of sumptuous repast' under the arches of the viaduct at Sheriff Street. Overhead, the first official train waited to depart for Drogheda and, in recognition of his contribution, Professor John MacNeill, the first professor of engineering at Trinity College, knelt down as plain 'John' and was elevated by the Lord Lieutenant as 'Sir John'.

MacNeill's engineering skills had been praised for finding solutions to apparently intractable problems and Dargan's team had put this to practical application. Between them, following the model of financial arrangements laid down by Pim, they had built a second railway line out of the city, this time running north along the coastal countryside leading to Drogheda.

Meantime, the UR was making its own gains, crabbing south-westwards out of Belfast. Portadown was reached in September 1842, two years before the D&DR had reached Drogheda. The UR had its sights set on extending to Armagh, as per its original plan. Before that could happen, it ran into a difficulty which illustrated the kinds of obstacles endemic to railway planning of that time.

The basic problem was that the powers granted in the original Act of Parliament for the extension to Armagh had lapsed. They therefore had to be renewed, with all the delays that were involved in finding parliamentary time for the supplementary legislation. The problem was not resolved until the spring of 1844. By then, the confidence of investors, already shaken, could not have been helped by the controversy over proposals to run the line on Sundays, which was provoked by Presbyterian ministers who condemned any activity which encroached upon the Sabbath. 'Sending souls to the Devil at Sixpence apiece' was how one preacher castigated the UR's intention to run a Sunday service.

Surviving clerical condemnation, the company agreed a dividend of $1\frac{1}{2}\%$ for the first year of operation. However, the social changes wrought by railway travel were unwelcome to some investors. In a class-bound era and in spite of the railways conveying cheap labour to their factories, some were taken aback by the extent to which railways facilitated 'the unwashed', as one director of UR put it. However, the gradual phasing in of third-class carriages facilitated the journeys of employees to the booming factories of Ulster's Industrial Revolution. In time, third-class travel would be upgraded from corralling passengers in goods wagons with bars on the sides.

Of much greater consequence was the disagreement over the gauges used by the respective companies—gauge being the distance between the running rails.

The D&KR had been built to the British gauge of 4 ft 8½ inches. The UR laid its rails to the gauge recommended by the Irish Railway Commissioners in their 1838 report; 6 ft 2 inches was the recommended measurement. The northerners had confidently built to that standard when the D&DR opted for a much narrower gauge of 5 ft 2 inches. This was the recommendation of their chief engineer, Sir John MacNeill, who argued that it would be cheaper to build.

It did not take a mathematician to work out that such savings would run into the sand at the point where the D&DR met the UR. Again, obstinacy ensued, with neither side willing to concede to the other's gauge. The D&DR company held that UR should concede to the southern standard and change all their lines, so that through-trains could run in both directions. The UR naturally countered that the Dublin company should adopt the Ulster measurement. Faced with such impasse between north and south, the Board of Trade was forced to arbitrate, appointing Major-General Pasley of the Royal Engineers to conduct an inquiry.

It was no accident that an army officer was chosen. Even though many of the engineers of the first railways had a military pedigree, the government prudently removed the arbitration of standards from among the competing companies and gave it to the Board of Trade, who recruited officers from the Royal Engineers to carry out the work.

Major-General Pasley took evidence from engineers north and south and from Britain, hearing arguments for a multiplicity of gauges but concluding that an acceptable gauge for Ireland lay somewhere between 5 ft and 5 ft 6 inches. He split the difference, recommending a gauge of 5 ft 3 inches, in what a later engineer described as 'an exercise in advanced mathematics'. Interestingly enough, 5 ft 3 inches is 1.600m in metric, one of the rare dimensions that qualifies as a 'round number' in both imperial and metric measures. That gauge remains one which Ireland shares with only a few countries.

The UR was put to considerable expense because of the recommendation. Their accounts show that nearly £20,000 (equivalent to £1m) was spent on the change-over. In April 1843, the Board of Trade acknowledged that the UR should be compensated by other companies who would benefit from the conversion. A clause to this effect was written into several Railway Acts passed from 1850.

The UR began to change its gauge in 1845. The earthworks of the line to Portadown had been built to take double tracks, but only one line of rails had been laid. The company laid a second line, built to the new 5 ft 3 inch gauge, alongside the original rails. This enabled the conversion to take place without disruption to normal services. By September 1847 the entire traffic of the line was being carried on the 5 ft 3 inch gauge.

(Public Record Office of Northern Ireland)

The Armagh railway disaster of 12 June 1889 was the worst in Irish railway history. Eighty died and nearly 400 were injured when the engine of an excursion train stalled near Dobbin's Bridge, just short of the summit of the incline out of Armagh station. The engine was uncoupled and the train was divided, but during this process the front part of the train reversed into the rear section. This began to roll out of control, down the gradient, and smashed into the oncoming Armagh to Newry train. The train had been chartered to carry a Methodist Sunday school from Armagh on an excursion to Warrenpoint.

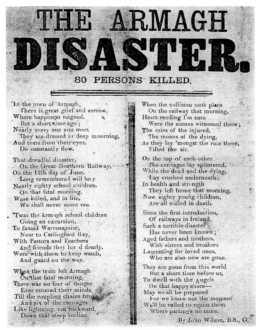

35

A legacy of this change can still be seen in the construction of parts of the northern railroad. Interestingly enough, much of it was built by William Dargan, who also built much of the D&DR, but to different standards of finish. Apart from pique at being forced to change its gauge, the future of the northern lines lay with 5 ft 3 inches. This became the gauge on the line to Armagh, which was reached early in 1848, having bridged the River Bann. As we shall see, bridging rivers and gorges became a feature of the Ulster lines, demonstrating considerable ingenuity in overcoming obstacles.

While all this was going on, other developments were being constructed piecemeal across Ulster. It appears that there was no grand plan, rather many individual lines promoted by companies which sought investors and parliamentary permission to connect Londonderry with Omagh, Omagh with Enniskillen and Cavan, Cavan with Newry, Newry with Dundalk, and Dundalk with Drogheda.

Which is where we left the D&DR, whose push northwards to meet the UR—which was crabbing south-west to Armagh—was already revealing on the map a notional spine between the two dominant cities of the island. But again, there was no grand plan in operation, rather the efforts of individual companies to build railway lines to specific destinations—the UR went from Belfast to Armagh, the D&DR between Dublin and Drogheda, while the 56-mile gap between Drogheda and Portadown would be filled by another entrant to the scene, the Dublin & Belfast Junction Railway. The D&BJR would be incorporated by Act of Parliament in 1845 and from this would emerge a rail connection between two distinctly different cultures on the island.

The trauma of the Great Famine was to have an impact even upon railway building. The chronicle of collective suffering is well documented elsewhere. To examine some of the effects of—and upon—the railways is not to diminish the wider impact, but to observe the role which the railways played in the wider context of human mobility.

The unpalatable fact is that, at the height of this 'technological advance', the greatest potential for bulk transport of food which the country had ever known— the railways—were used, not to alleviate mass hunger, but rather as a means of mass exodus. Any possible benefits of the railway were seen in terms of giving employment rather than of moving food. If a grand plan of relief by rail existed in some cupboard in Dublin Castle, it was not communicated to the individual companies. They were sometimes intimidated into taking on more men, in order that they might feed their families. O'Connell had seen the railway companies' need for labour as a means of alleviating the distressed. There is evidence that Dargan took on more labour than he needed in stricken districts.

This photograph was taken in Belfast on Ulster Day, 28 September 1912. It shows the massive crowd assembled to sign the Ulster Solemn League and Covenant. The development of the railways in the second half of the nineteenth century facilitated the movement of large crowds for recreational, political or vocational purposes. (Ulster Museum)

Craigmore Viaduct. A curving incline over eighteen arches. (National Library of Ireland)

James Barton.
(Canice O'Mahoney)

Famine apart, and at the time there was no full comprehension of either its geographic scale or severity, the railway companies continued building their separate lines between Belfast and Dublin.

By 1844, the D&DR company had achieved its goal of a terminus in Drogheda. Four years later, the UR had reached Armagh. A glaring gap was now apparent between Drogheda and Armagh. However, a problem lay at the southern end, at Drogheda, where the deep gorge of the Boyne would have to be spanned.

As we have seen, the D&BJR was empowered to fill the gap between Drogheda and Portadown. This would be the crucial leg, connecting the important towns of Dundalk and Newry and—with one other smaller gap yet to be linked—providing the rail link on the 56-mile stretch along the coast. The last gasp of the inland route was a scheme of 1845, backed by the UR board, called the Dublin & Armagh Inland Railway. It was planned to connect with the original UR's plan for an 'inland' route out of Belfast, via Armagh, Navan and Kells, to Dublin. There were plans for a branch line from Navan to Drogheda to link with the D&BJR. However, the D&AIR went under in the 1846 slump.

Again, we see the landed classes, merchants and bankers investing, though the imminence of famine and potential unrest, combined with the difficulties anticipated in the construction work, contributed to a slow uptake of shares. Nevertheless, work progressed with even greater numbers than hitherto. When the two lines were simultaneously being constructed, the main and the branch line, upwards of 3,000 labouring men were working. Apart from the cuttings and embankments, the most spectacular constructions were the viaducts.

The route was worked on simultaneously at several locations—often miles apart—dictated by decisions as to the stretches that would require a longer lead-in time to actual excavation. When the time came for testing a locomotive, it was important that there should not be hold-ups because of additional digging or shuttering. Building viaducts clearly required more groundworks on either side than, say, embankments or cuttings.

Dargan's team, which had been heading south from Portadown, did some extraordinary work across marshland towards Mullaghglass and Goraghwood. A viaduct was needed to get across the Newry Valley, and the village of Bessbrook was used as a base camp. The building of the Craigmore Viaduct was a saga in itself, but, when we look upon it today, with its spanning arches supporting an 'even curving incline of the permanent way', it is worth remembering that it was built without benefit of machinery or earth-moving equipment, without computer models or test laboratories. Its design was the product of nineteenth-century mathematics and its execution a monument to Dargan's abilities. It was delivered by the confident expertise of his engineers and workmen, who had but 'brick to build with and granite to build upon' (although, to be accurate, it is made of stone).

Emboldened by the building of Craigmore Viaduct (Craigmore means the Big Rock), the company set about a much greater challenge. With the linking of several lines now in sight, the building of a railway bridge across the Boyne Valley would allow access between Dublin and Belfast on the coastal route. Until the building of the viaduct over the Boyne, passengers had to alight from the train and proceed on foot through the streets of Drogheda from the terminus of the D&DR to the D&BJR station at Newfoundwell, on the northern side of the Boyne. Bridging the Boyne would make one through line.

Such was the engineering challenge, the commitment of labour, finance and materials, that practically error-free models had to be constructed. MacNeill, who was now consultant engineer to the D&BJR, had overseen much of this work and advanced his specifications for the viaduct. These were amended by the company's chief engineer, James Barton, who found serious deficiencies in the load-bearing calculations. The Department of Engineering at Trinity College was invoked to resolve the differences between the two eminent engineers. Their calculations appear to vindicate Barton, calling for strengthening of the lattice girders sufficient to bear locomotives and carriages with a combined weight of 1,000 tons—the weight of two full trains passing each other at the centre of the structure. (It was not envisaged that such dual traffic over the bridge would normally be the case, but prudence in allowing for such a possibility was the hallmark of the Board of Trade inspectors.)

It was a massive undertaking. Workmen died, money ran out, a contractor went bankrupt. The central span stretched to 226 feet on two piers whose foundations went 30 feet underwater, into alluvial clay which had to be shuttered and excavated by chain bucket. The very depth of the gouged and worn Boyne Valley indicated the softness of the river bed and the immensity of the challenge. The viaduct took the best part of ten years to build, from planning to completion.

When the massive lattice girder bridge was completed in 1852 it was the wonder of railway building. But, with the outer support of wooden scaffolding still in place, it induced nervousness in the very customers for whom so much had been ventured. The paying passengers preferred to leave the train before it went over the viaduct and to make their way by the traditional road bridge to resume their train journey on the other side.

At the time, much that was happening in the wider world gave cause for unease. Famine and civil disorder had been increasing since the connection

Drogheda and the Boyne Viaduct. View from the bridge.   (Ulster Museum)

Work on reconstructing the Viaduct in the early 1930s.

Crossing the Boyne.
The original double-
track bridge dating
from 1855 (above).
The construction of the
Boyne Viaduct in the
1850s was the greatest
single engineering
achievement in the
construction of the
Dublin to Belfast
railway link. The
bridge was rebuilt in
the early 1930s,
without disrupting
traffic, as a single-
track structure able to
take much heavier
locomotives.

*Beside the seaside.
These photographs of
Whitehead, County
Antrim, show the
effect of the railways
on the development of
seaside resorts.
A similar process
occurred in many
parts of the island,
notably Bray, County
Wicklow, Tramore,
County Waterford,
and Portrush, County
Antrim. (National
Library of Ireland)*

between the two cities was mooted. From the deep south-west came reports of attacks upon railway personnel by starving peasantry and threats to the civil order, upon which the railways depended for their financing. Undoubtedly the state of the country mitigated against the celebration of the Boyne Viaduct, which was a huge advance in transport links between the south and north.

Despite the fact that many navvies went off to soldier in the Crimean War—and finished up building railways as part of the war effort—the Boyne Viaduct was completed by 1855. This finally made the railway viable from Dublin along the east coast to Belfast. The completion provoked a renewed interest in making subsidiary lines, which soon spread out inland from the major towns along the way. Over the next half-century, the railways would snake across Ulster from that first connection between the two dominant cities, bringing the railway to remote parts of the province.

CHAPTER THREE

The Great Southern & Western— The Premier Line

Heuston station today retains a nineteenth-century façade wrapped around a twentieth-century railway terminus which caters for a multiplicity of traveller needs. It is the rail gateway to the south-west, the place that has defined Dublin for generations of migrants who continue to swell the ever-increasing population of the metropolis.

It is both a cultural marker and a demographic totem of the imbalance between the capital and the country, of the flight from the land to the congested capital of traffic gridlock and personal opportunity. It has been so since the late 1840s, when the Great Southern & Western Railway became the third main railway to open on the island and effected a profound change in mobility upon a rural population.

Although the terminus building of Kingsbridge was not finished when the journeyman journalist Alexander Somerville saw it in 1847, he correctly predicted it would become 'regal in magnificence'. By the standards of the time, the same might be said of the completed line. Somerville had come to Ireland to report on the Famine for a Manchester newspaper and travelled the first fifty miles of his journey on the new railway line of the GS&WR, which had recently completed that distance as far as Carlow.

The Kingsbridge terminus from which he started his journey out of Dublin was on the west side of the city, adjacent to the river. Designed by the architect Sancton Wood, its classical appearance pleased the directors of the GS&WR and reflected some of their ambitions for the line. Even so, they could hardly have forecast the extent to which the route, when completed, would imprint itself upon a century and a half of Irish life.

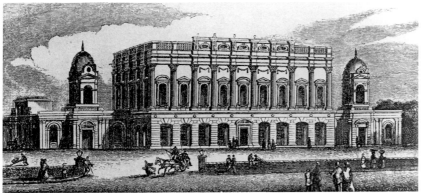

Kingsbridge station, head office of the Great Southern & Western Railway. Designed by Sancton Wood in an open competition, the ambitious design encountered labour problems and took years to finish. By 1847 the railway line was in operation, but the terminus building was not completed. Looking like a 'Medici palace next to Guinness' brewery', it was described by the architectural historian Maurice Craig as 'a Renaissance Palazzo, gay and full-blooded, with fruity swags and little domed towers on the wings, a formal composition, excellently articulated'. On the parapet of the stone castings are the hereditary arms of the cities of Dublin, Cork and Limerick, all served by the GS&WR.

The great achievement of the GS&WR was to link the cities of Dublin (above, National Gallery of Ireland) and Cork (right, National Library of Ireland) by the middle of the nineteenth century.

The GS&WR was to become Ireland's biggest railway company, carrying the most passengers and having the largest amount of rolling stock. It was to spawn branch lines over a good part of the south and west of the island, providing railway travel to all but the most remote districts. As a conduit of mobility from the countryside to the city, the GS&WR was to become inextricably bound to the politics and evolution of the island. Perversely, the first material function of the line was to engage in mass exportation of potential customers.

Completed in the bleak mid-century of famine hunger, it provided the first leg of outward carriage for refugees, taking passengers to ports for the New World, setting in place a continuum of migration to be forever identified with railways. In a later Ireland it would bring to the capital young recruits to the civil service and activists to the political ferment of the fledgling twentieth-century state. If its beginnings in the mid-nineteenth century helped depopulate a demoralised country, a hundred years on in the mid-twentieth century it was destined to help revive and modernise it.

Without the GS&WR, thousands of starving refugees would never have made their escape from famine, while in the early twentieth century it facilitated the need of the growing capital to have a ready feedstock of educated youth from the regions. By the same tracks that decanted hungry townlands into the ports in the 1850s came, a century later, recruits to the army, police and to business, whose careers of 'upward mobility' would start along a rail line authorised by an Act passed by parliament in 1844.

The politically fractious Ireland of the mid-nineteenth century was rapidly developing into volatile disarray, with the movement for Repeal of the Union, led by Daniel O'Connell, gaining popular support. Monster meetings heard how the Union had failed to improve the welfare of a population which was in the grip of a fertility boom yet was tied to a system of land tenure which could not feed that population. The land system required constant sub-division into smallholdings whose produce just about paid the rent, leaving little to cope with the persistent crop failures which occurred throughout the 1800s.

Whether there was a natural process of compensation for the many deaths from the eight outbreaks of famine between 1800 and 1840, or a process of natural selection in the wake of such depletion, the population peaked to over eight million in the 1840s, putting such a strain on resources that armed police were constantly having to cope with outbreaks of disorder and the murder of landlords' agents. Alexander Somerville, whose own background was of rural poverty in England, read of 5,000 troops being sent to Clonmel and was able to see for himself how desperate was the situation as he rode in the new rail coaches from Dublin on the GS&WR in January 1847. He dispatched the following to a Manchester newspaper:

The enmity of Protestant and Catholic led the first, he being usually the landlord, to allow the latter, the potato-eating tenant, to get in arrear, that might be at any time evicted by means of the law, when a better tenant offered for the land. The Protestant landlord, having all the law on his side—all the officials being Protestants, from the Lord-Lieutenant to the hangman—he was seldom particular about the moral justice of such cases. There were armed police ever at hand to help the landlord, if the tenant did not yield possessions, and betake himself to a ditch, to lie and die quietly.

Compared to living conditions in the English counties, of which he had vast experience, Somerville remarked upon the prevalence of armed police: 'whom one meets on every road, in every village. Even on the farm land they have belts and pouches, ball cartridges in the pouches, short guns called carbines and bayonets and pistols and swords.' He noted that the military went about less armed.

At the height of this political maelstrom, the promoters planned a line from Dublin to Cork, built in stages to connect with other lines planned for Kilkenny, with a spur to the busy port of Waterford on the south coast. This scheme, which was well advanced by 1847, was planned by the companies in England, who saw the rail momentum from Manchester and Liverpool continuing across the Irish Sea in their own steamships and then by a rail route inland to the south-west, which, even then, was notable for the visitor attractions of Killarney and the commerce of Cork.

According to historian Joe Lee, the various railway proposals of the British companies were scrutinised by the Tory Prime Minister, Robert Peel, with an eye to easing famine unrest. Peel hoped railways would give employment to men and feed families, thereby taking the pressure off his government. Peel was familiar with the volatility of Irish life under English rule, having begun his career when his father purchased for him the parliamentary seat of Cashel in County Tipperary. He became Chief Secretary for Ireland in 1812, at the age of 24. He was in his second term as Prime Minister of the 'United' Kingdom when famine struck again in Ireland, more widespread and devastating than before. By then he was in his late fifties.

Peel seized upon the railway plans, encouraging changes of route which would give a branch to Carlow and continue to Cashel in Tipperary, then the most disturbed county in Ireland. Tipperary was being called a 'slaughterhouse county' by the *Freeman's Journal* newspaper, such was the extent of death from hunger, disease and the consequent violence against the landlords' agents. The Lord Lieutenant of Ireland, Lord Clarendon, had refused several invitations from well-meaning farming co-operatives to visit Tipperary in case, as one report put it, he would 'get a ball through his greatcoat'.

With the promoters of the London & Birmingham company, with whom he was connected by patronage, Peel looked further at a rail system that would open up the countryside outside of 'The Pale', make Tipperary amenable to work and policing and ultimately arrive in Cork, capital of the south. Along the way it would convert to rail travel a substantial section of rural Ireland, showing the practical value of the Union (which was constantly being assailed by nationalists). The line would proceed along the south-west coast, where plans were mooted for transatlantic liners to berth in deep-water harbours in counties Kerry and Cork (similar plans had been proposed for the western port of Galway).

For those less enamoured with the Union, the railway would facilitate their emigration. For the nationalist middle classes—whose patience, though strained, had not yet snapped—it brought some good at a time when food prices were rising and famine was rampant. When the Irish parliament had amalgamated with the British as part of the Act of Union in 1801, the more business-minded landlords and some of the rural merchant class had abandoned their Irish holdings to the care of agents and focused their interests nearer Westminster.

The directors of the GS&WR were more concerned with making a railroad than with the political unrest. At Peel's behest, the board of the L&BR lent the GS&WR the sum of half a million pounds in 1847 and this injection of capital helped to complete the line. The GS&WR directors wanted a railway which would emulate the great achievement of the L&BR.

England had about 2,000 miles of main line at this time and Ireland had about 70 miles, so from the point of view of the L&BR Ireland seemed fertile territory for expansion. The start-up costs (about £15m in today's prices) included subscriptions from shareholders of the L&BR, among them the prominent financier J. P. Boothby and the banking brokers Pierse and Casanove who raised the substantial 'seed' money. In Ireland the Quaker investor, James Perry, and the owner of a horse-drawn coach service, Peter Purcell, were the main movers.

As the land survey was nearing completion, the War Department lobbied to have a station near the expansive plains of the Curragh in Kildare, where the bulk of military training and manoeuvres took place. Members of parliament who voted for the GS&WR expected it to run through their constituencies, while the coaching interests who had invested in the company wanted stops at towns which were already served by their own routes. After some amendments to the Act and new surveys by the engineers of changes in the original route (for instance, the route would now pass west of Cashel rather than east), the first sod was ceremoniously dug by the Duke of Leinster at Adamstown, near Lucan, in January 1845.

Sir Robert Peel, from an original drawing of 1836 by Sir Thomas Lawrence PRA. (Hulton Getty)

'Father of the Railways'. A bust of William Dargan by John E. Jones. (National Gallery of Ireland)

According to one account, 'His Grace took off his coat and in his shirtsleeves dug up six sods which he threw into a wheelbarrow . . .', provoking one onlooker to say that he could now die happy as he had seen a duke working like any common man. The Duke of Leinster was an extensive landowner and the new line would run through his property, for which he expected to be repaid with profits. The way the company worked was to invite bids or tenders for the 'divisions' of the line, which the successful contractor would in time sub-contract to another builder for smaller stretches.

With the successful Dublin to Kingstown line behind him and while simultaneously engaged in building parts of the Dublin to Drogheda line, William Dargan shared the contract for this first stretch of the GS&WR, making sufficient progress in six months for the directors to ride over a completed section between Lucan and Sallins. By the summer of 1846, as the newspapers were reporting widespread distress from the failure of the potato crop, the next leg to Carlow was complete.

The journey from Dublin to Carlow took about two and a half hours, averaging 22 mph, three times the speed of the stagecoach. The carriages were revolutionary in terms of comfort: the first-class carriages had upholstered seats with arm rests and a décor similar to a Victorian drawing-room, the whole lit by suspended oil lamps.

In winter passengers could hire foot warmers and in summer picnic hampers. Travelling on the line in January 1847, six months after the opening, Somerville noted that:

> The carriages are well fitted-up and more roomy than on the English narrow gauge lines—the Irish railways being a medium gauge between the narrow and the broad, and going so steadily as to make the passenger think he is sitting in a parlour.

Going through Kildare he noted:

> The surface of the country on both sides of the railway is nearly dead level all the way . . . it feeds cattle and sheep and furnishes hay for Dublin. Several elegant villas and mansions are seen and a good many humble dwelling-places.

Profoundly political, Somerville also recorded that there was 'no land which seemed to have been in corn and potato fields . . .' two-thirds of that country is lying in grass'. He saw the extensive pastures of County Kildare laid out for livestock, which the Catholic poor could not afford. By the time he arrived in Carlow, he heard that:

> *Awful havoc was made among the small tenantry, in getting them cleared away to make large farms and to substitute a Protestant population for a Catholic one. Carlow town and county is a stronghold of the political Protestants. The land is free fertile loam, which grows prodigious crops of onions. London is sometimes supplied with Carlow onions.*

As to the railway, he was assured it was giving employment at the rate of '100 men per mile'. Somerville cites William Dargan as having 30,000 men employed on his various contracts. Somerville is unable to ascertain their wages, but promises 'to reach that important branch of information soon'. (It was not surprising that he met with difficulty in discovering the level of earnings. The emergency poor law relief provided a daily subsistence which men working on the railway would lose if it were shown they earned more than the relief rate. Dargan was paying a shilling a day for basic labouring, a valuable few pence more than the relief rate.)

In Carlow, Somerville observed that the stagecoaches met the train from Dublin. Far from being made redundant by the first line into that part of the country, the stagecoaches were invested with a new importance by providing feeder routes from the terminus at Carlow to Clonmel, Kilkenny, Waterford and Cork. Most of these coaches were provided by Charles Bianconi, an Italian immigrant who had prospered in the wake of the British victory at Waterloo, which had reduced the export of horses from Ireland for the army. Bianconi was able to take up the surplus horses at low cost to service his coaching routes.

As far back as 1830 he had bought stock in the Waterford to Limerick railway route, the first line to be authorised. Although the plans of the W&LR lay in abeyance, Bianconi maintained his interest by providing regular coach services to connect with the GS&WR, drawn from his supply of 70 coaches and 1,000 horses which he maintained at Clonmel, where he was familiarly known as 'Brian Cooney'.

With Carlow established as the rail bridgehead, Bianconi's coaches ran feeder services through outlying townlands in counties Waterford, Kilkenny, Tipperary, King's County (Offaly) and Queen's County (Laois). The increased travel gave a fillip to local commerce and helped trade in vegetables, butter and milk to Dublin but seems not to have been able to alleviate the Famine, which was traumatising the countryside even as the railway was making it accessible.

We need not here be diverted into a treatise on the Famine, other than to record the relative failure of the government to use the southern railways, by then the greatest experiment in mass mobility, to transport food relief. (Large quantities of grain imported for Famine relief were transported by the Ulster Railway from Belfast to Armagh between 1847 and 1848). Instead, even as the GS&WR was

A fully laden stagecoach
going at full gallop in the
mid-nineteenth century.
With 4,000 miles of routes,
Bianconi's coaches provided
'feeder-services' to the
railway in the south.

Charles
Bianconi.

making its mark upon the landscape, millions of pounds' worth of meal was leaving the country by convoys of horses and carts, which were accompanied to the ports by armed escort.

Waiting at his hotel in Carlow for the coach from the railway station, the writer for the *Manchester Examiner* observed:

Already the professional mendicants are assembling outside the door to besiege the coaches . . . muffled up in tattered cloaks, greatcoats and all manner of garments slung, hung, wrapped, twisted and tied upon them . . . fifteen or sixteen have arrived to unfold to the public eye their sores, which form their stock in trade . . . 'Oh, it will be the lucky day to your honour if you give me handsel . . . Give something to the poor, for God's sake.'

The coaches begin to arrive from the railway. The mob of beggars rush to the windows of the coaches . . . when they see a lady and gentleman together, they assume that she is his wife and may be in the family way. Before her eyes they open their hideous sores, and beg of the gentleman, for the love of God, to give them something. I get upon the box-seat of the Clonmel coach. 'Oh your honour has got the box-seat, you'll give us a handsel: do, for the love of God, give something to the poor. Give the poor creatures of women a handsel, and it will be the lucky day to you' . . . A gentleman, mounted on a fine hunter, with scarlet coat and booted and spurred, living close to Carlow, returns from the hunt and rides through the crowd. A passenger asks why don't they beg from him. 'From him is it,' they reply, 'Sure we know him better, it would not be a ha-penny he would give the likes of us.'

Two years before, the Riot Act was read to disperse a crowd of starving and unemployed men who were blockading the export of grain from the port of Dungarvan in County Waterford. When the blockade continued, a detachment of dragoons fired on the men, killing two and wounding several.

Although the government did not use the railways to carry relief food, it did endeavour to pass bills through parliament more speedily in order to provide employment. A job on the railway was no longer a matter of improving one's earnings. If a man failed to get into the workhouse, or 'Union', a railway job was the difference between life and death, as a labourer could earn enough to feed himself and his family.

As the line advanced into north Tipperary, political agitation was widespread as a result of large-scale starvation. Although some landlords dispensed food and went without rent, often leading to bankruptcy (in one rare case a landlord gave over his mansion to the hungry), many set their face against helping the poor. Bailiffs continued to demand rent from tenant farmers who could no longer pay, as their smallholdings were poisoned with potato blight.

Charity dispensed to starving people. The horror of the Great Famine led to pathetic scenes throughout the country. All the while, construction of the railway went ahead, although not without much unrest along the way. (Illustrated London News)

The opening of the Cork and Kinsale junction railway in County Cork in 1863 and the arrival of the first train at Kinsale. The major part of the Irish railway network had been completed, but spur routes such as this continued to be built throughout the second half of the nineteenth century. (Illustrated London News)

Amidst scenes of widespread distress, with emaciated tenants being evicted onto the roadside or to emergency 'poor houses', a movement of political resistance—and revenge—gained rapid ground. Landlords and their agents were shot, cattle had their hind legs cut off (the blood and limbs were taken away for broiling for nourishment) and hauliers of crops were attacked.

Responding to their need, William Dargan took on more men than the work required, some of whom had spent the previous months building stone walls around the estates of the landlords (man-traps were sometimes set inside these estates, steel contraptions which were capable of cutting an interloper in half). Secret societies of 'Ribbonmen' attacked railway stores, foremen were threatened, and Dargan gave instructions that more labourers be taken on and urged the directors to pressure government for a subsidy.

The railways were seen as being on the side of the oppressive class. They had been financed by the merchants and bankers, and favoured stops in places convenient for landlords and their retinues, whose extravagant social activities were hardly curtailed by the starvation at their gates. The *Freeman's Journal* during that period reported banquets and social events side by side with random death from 'waste', as the starvation was described.

As the unrest increased, so did attacks on the rail works. Wooden sleepers and lengths of iron rail were stolen, and it was feared that they would be fashioned into weaponry. The radical, John Mitchell, had urged the destitute to smelt down the rails into the primitive 'pike' of agrarian attack and split railway sleepers into pike handles.

Armed police guarded the blasting powder which was used for tunnelling and rock breaking. The advance of the railway into Tipperary took on an air of siege, with the work continuing under military protection. Near Ballybrophy a ganger was murdered—he had refused to hire hungry men from a local family—whereupon Dargan issued a notice that, if the intimidation did not cease, he would cease building the railway. Attacks on railway property eased and, in spite of the debilitated state of the additional labour, the line made headway to a point in south Tipperary where the new Waterford to Limerick line had arrived at a notional terminus two months before.

It was named Tipperary Junction—later to become Limerick Junction (despite being in County Tipperary)—and was strategically located 22 miles from Limerick, where the line from Dublin crossed the Waterford–Limerick line, thereby connecting Dublin with Limerick city, from whence travellers could go by boat downstream along the Shannon to Tarbert Island on the estuary and thence into Kerry. Similarly, from 1854 onwards when the W&L line was completed, trains from Waterford could connect with Limerick Junction and have access to Kerry in the same way. In spite of the wretched state of the poorer population, the GS&WR had provided the makings of modern tourism from Britain to Killarney, part of the wider plan of the shareholding of the L&BR to promote tourist travel to Ireland.

It had taken three years to build the 107 miles to Limerick Junction, at a cost favourable to the investors in hostile local conditions. Dargan had recourse to the newspapers to rebut charges of exploitation and poor wages, noting that since he began building railways in Ireland:

> *I have paid upwards of £800,000 in wages and have never in any instance, either directly or indirectly, connected myself with the truck system, or knowingly permitted any person employed by me to have recourse to it.*

As noted in the last chapter, the 'truck system', which was prevalent in England, was a kind of company store run as a monopoly by contractors, purveying goods and implements at inflated prices or in lieu of wages to the navvies. Making the point that he paid a minimum of 1s 6d per day—high wages for the time—William Dargan and the directors might have been well pleased with themselves in getting that much of the line laid, but the reality of 'the most distressful country' was uppermost when Lord Clarendon, the Lord Lieutenant, agreed to officiate at the opening ceremony.

Tipperary was a hotbed of political unrest and, in the view of some Dublin Castle officials, the least safe place for the Lord Lieutenant to travel, an opinion shared by Clarendon, then object of universal hatred among the peasantry. In Dublin, in spite of thousands of troops in the streets and the added fortification of the Castle, Clarendon regarded himself as 'nearly a State prisoner', a description which he wrote in a letter to Lord John Russell, complaining that he could only venture outside the Castle 'for a short walk in the Park', such were the threats to his life. 'No Tipperary landlord ever received more threatening notices than I do . . . as to when and where I am to be assassinated' he wrote, having sent his children to England for safety. Yet that was the county he would now visit, because of a government loan of £500,000 to the railway whose landmark junction in Tipperary was seen as sufficiently important to show investors that the country was safe.

Protected by a detachment of militia, he attended a banquet at the mansion of Lord Hawarden, the estate cordoned off by cavalry. During a stage-managed event at Limerick Junction, workmen were paid a shilling to swell the crowd and cheer. According to one report in the nationalist *Freeman's Journal*, the navvies 'gave one of the most consumptive cheers ever heard by His Excellency but a real Tipperary cheer for the patriot John Mitchel'.

One is tempted to read into that report that, in starving times, they had 'taken the shilling' not as a recruitment bounty to the army but to applaud 'with faint cheers' the figure of government whilst showing their genuine feelings for their rebellious hero, whom Clarendon had jailed a few months before under coercion laws to quell famine unrest. Mitchell had long urged outright armed rebellion against English rule. His sentence of transportation to Tasmania for fourteen years had provoked widespread unrest and was to lead to the badly organised rebellion of Young Irelanders within weeks of Clarendon's Tipperary visit.

From the vantage point of the GS&WR, getting to Limerick Junction and creating a connection with the Waterford to Limerick line proved to be strategically important for the subsequent development of the company. Controlling 'The Junction' (as it would be known) provided them with a staging post to continue southwards to Cork and Kerry, to cross the Shannon above Limerick and access the western counties and, in time, to build a line up the entire west coast, from Limerick to Sligo.

However, that was very much in the future when, in 1849, Dargan was negotiating a further subsidy from the government to enable him to give relief employment and to continue the line southwards to Buttevant, another garrison town. Beyond that was Mallow, a substantial market town which, two years before, was described as 'a countryside in the grip of a peasant economy, with intense pressure of population'.

To build across the undulating country of high hills and slopes to Mallow from Buttevant required casting a continuous gradient over the best part of seven miles, supported by embankments whose infill demanded 1,000 cubic yards of muck per day. Thousands of tons were taken from the tops of hills to be dumped between the hills as levelling—then thousands more yards of hard-core and earth were carried and shaped into embankments, on which the railway would then be built. Before it could be 'built', however, the embankments had to be finished off with a top layer of stones and shale, stamped down by dozens of labourers marching along it until it was compacted into a bed upon which wooden sleepers could be laid to support the rails.

With the extra men taken on for famine relief, night work was carried on by the light of paraffin and tar barrels, which must have been some sight across a pastoral countryside. This 'division' of the line—from Buttevant to Mallow—was the sixth of nine divisions from Thurles to Cork, the entire 78 miles being the longest contract so far undertaken by Dargan. In September 1948, the chief engineer, Sir John MacNeill, was able to report to his board that 'the earthworks

The GS&WR ran through the agricultural heartland of the south of Ireland and played a vital part in the development of the rural economy. The produce of creameries and fairs was transported to local railheads for national distribution.

are in a very forward state'. MacNeill elaborated that '1,000 cubic yards of stuff per day from the side cutting and from Goolds Hills and Walsh's Hill have been run into it'.

To understand the reality of that engineering feat, it is worth citing railway historian Terry Coleman's account of making cuttings:

> In embanking the aim was always to extract the necessary soil from the nearest possible place and the engineers would have allowed for this when they first surveyed the way . . . this was done by tipping. A light tram road was made from the cutting to the edge of the embankment and at the extreme edge a stout piece of timber was fastened to prevent wagons toppling over the edge when they discharged their contents. A train of loaded trucks was then brought up to within fifty yards of the edge. The first truck was detached from the train and a horse hitched to it. The horse then drew the wagon, walked not directly in front of it between tram lines but to the side as if it were a canal horse on a towpath drawing a barge behind and to its side.
>
> The horse was made to walk, then trot and then gallop. When the truck got near the embankment edge the man running the horse detached its halter, gave it a signal it had been taught to obey and horse and man leaped aside. But the truck continued until it struck the baulk of wood laid across the end of the track, when it tipped forward, ejecting its contents over the edge of the bank. The horse was immediately brought up again and hooked on, and the truck was righted and drawn away.

'Tipping' clearly required considerable dexterity with horse and truck, and the horse-handlers were often adolescents. The shaping and tapering was then done by the navvies with shovels, to the instructions of the gangers, who in turn were working to the engineers who assessed the gradient or 'the line of the rise'. Much of the heavy work of blasting and excavating was hazardous, but it would be Dargan's boast, as the last stretch of heavy banking into Mallow was completed, that it had been free of loss of life (there was no mention of limbs).

As Mallow was an important trading town and a junction in its own right for roads into Munster, the company decided on a station that would be a showpiece of railway architecture for the time: Gothic-Baroque, with turrets, tall chimneys and an overhanging canopy that was much admired, not least for its primary purpose of giving shelter. With the station finished to become the temporary terminus of the line—a mere two weeks behind schedule—the opening was celebrated in the *Illustrated London News*, which noted it had taken place on 17 March:

The GS&WR engine, number 36, built in 1847 by Bury, Curtis and Kennedy, and withdrawn in 1875, was later preserved and is now on display in the foyer of Cork's Kent station. It is the oldest surviving Irish railway locomotive by a long way.

[The opening] was an event fraught with so much importance to the public of Mallow and the surrounding localities, calculated to affect so materially their future conditions and interests . . . that the streets and thoroughfares were crowded by thousands of all classes, thronging onto the terminus to behold the great, and, to many of them, the astounding innovation.

The *Illustrated London News* reported on the excitement, which threatened to get out of hand: 'When 2 o'clock arrived, as did *no* train, disappointment was giving way to insubordination.' However, the eventual arrival provoked:

. . . a tremendous cheering and waving of hats . . . On, on it came, the great engine panting and hissing, screeching and fuming, whilst the peasantry cheered or stood mute in wonder, occasionally uttering ejaculations of surprise and astonishment.

The arrival of 'a goodly train of carriages, well filled, yoked to the engines', produced further lyrical passages:

Amidst loud and protracted cheering on came the locomotive steaming rapidly and steadily to the terminus . . . amid increased acclamation from the multitude.

It had travelled the 145 miles from Dublin in about 5½ hours, stopping at 11 stations and making 30 mph on the level stretches, hugely impressive for the time. The banquet in the Mallow Hotel was regarded as generous, 'with cover laid for 150'. The Royal Toast was drunk, as was that of the directors of the GS&WR. 'The health of Mr Dargan was drunk—and that gentleman having returned thanks, the party broke up.'

A few days later in the Dublin headquarters at Kingsbridge station, now fully built, a board meeting acknowledged 'the persevering energy of their contractor Mr Dargan' for building to Mallow, 'notwithstanding a very unfavourable season for the execution of public works'. Locally it was recognised that Dargan's charity—or practical foresight—in taking men off the relief books had alleviated some of the famine hostility and ensured the railway's further passage to Cork.

This would require more building on a grand scale. To make a bridge across the River Blackwater required the building of a spectacular viaduct, one to rival that over the Boyne. South of Mallow station, a rising embankment was built, raising the already high natural banks of the river. Over 300,000 cubic yards of earth was brought by rail and by horse to build the incline from Mallow station to the river bank on the north side. Almost as much again was used to raise up the embankment on the south side, hauled mainly by horse and truck.

The Cork Exhibition of 1902 presented the wonders of the age, including the GS&WR's exhibit of engine and carriages built at the company's works in Inchicore, Dublin. (National Library of Ireland)

With work on both sides, the scaffolding was put in place for the respective abutments to the reinforced river banks. Between those abutments, or buttresses, foundations were embedded in the river to take nine piers supporting ten arches, the piers built up 20 feet 'to the springing of the arches', whose apex was another 40 feet above the river.

With the arch-sheeting being cut and dressed by 150 stonemasons on site, it required the combination of quantity surveying, classical engineering and traditional block building to deliver the bridge. Nothing like Mallow Viaduct had ever been seen in Munster. It excited the admiration of the building fraternity and the general public alike. It measured 515 feet across from buttress to buttress, the span of each arch being 45 feet. Apart from its visual impact, it showed how the railway builders could set their stamp upon a remote rural area when possessed of the money, ingenuity and labour to shape the landscape to the needs of the iron road.

One newspaper writer was moved to lyrical licence:

> Viewed from below the effect is particularly fine, the noble arches forming magnificent frames for as sweet pictures as could be seen, having all the rich tone of colouring belonging to this season in wood, stream, sky and background. The prevailing character of this, as of all the structures on the line, is an appearance of graceful lightness.

Mindful of the nervousness which the structure might induce, he went on to assure passengers that:

> . . . no works can be more substantial, the foundations being deeply sunk and the material being of the very best stone which the country affords.

With the Blackwater negotiated, more heavy work had to be done to reach Cork city, which lay within a protective valley at the cusp of the Lee estuary. Landward, Cork was surrounded by mountains, and to gain purchase along the slopes, prolonged and heavy blasting was required to make cuttings into the granite rock faces. On an uphill gradient to surmount the natural barrier of the high territory north of Cork city, Dargan was faced with making a cutting of almost a mile in length and 90 feet in depth. To get a sense of the labour involved in cutting into a mountainside, it is worth quoting Coleman again:

> On the face of the hill through which the cutting was to pass, bodies of men started work between the posts and rails which marked the intended line of the railway. The upper surface of the earth was carted away, and soon the hill was laid open and a

gullet excavated. This was a little cutting just large enough to take a row of wagons which were used to take the earth away. In this gullet the wagons could be brought alongside the navvies who were working on the banks above the temporary line. Meanwhile, as the muck was removed by the navvies on both sides, the gullet was continued into the hill by those ahead. This was the method used when the soil from the cutting was needed for an embankment farther along the line, to which stuff was carted in horse-drawn trains of wagons.

Sometimes, when there was no use for the soil, it had to be lifted up the sloping walls of the cutting and dumped at the top and sides. This was done by barrow runs, and 'making the running' was the most spectacular part of the navvy work and one of the most dangerous. The runs were made by laying planks up the side of the cutting, up which barrows wheeled. The running was performed by the strongest of the men. A rope, attached to the barrow and to each man's belt, ran up the side of the cutting and then round a pulley at the top, where it was attached to a horse. When the barrow was loaded, a signal was given to the horse-driver at the top and the man was drawn up the side of the cutting, balancing the barrow in front of him. If the horse pulled steadily and the man kept his balance everything went well. The man tipped his barrow load on to the top of the cutting, turned around and went down the side of the cutting again, this time drawing his barrow after him and with his back to it while the horse all the time kept the rope taut and took most of the weight of the empty barrow.

But, if on the upward climb the horse slipped or if the man lost his balance on the muddy plank, then he had to save himself by throwing the loaded barrow to one side and himself to the other.

At this remove one can only imagine the collective labour of the navvies in making the mile-long cutting. Dargan had set himself six months to get from Mallow to the outskirts of Cork at Kilbarry. Because of the hilly nature of the terrain, with tributary rivers to be forded, the line was almost a continuous series of gradients through rock cuttings, bridges over rivers, and elongated earthworks to carry embankments. Thousands of navvies, working day and night, tons of blasting powder, hundreds of horses pulling thousands of cubic yards of muck—it was truly the mastering of the hilly land north of Cork city.

Two more viaducts were completed in three months. Monard Viaduct measured 360 feet from buttress to buttress, across eight arches, while that at Kilnap was 412 feet in length and had an elevation of 108 feet. The rail ran with a curve on a rising gradient of 1:60. The Act authorising the line stipulated that Cork station should be built:

This engine,
number 260,
built in
1913, served
the GS&WR
and its
successor
company, the
Great
Southern
Railway, for
many years.
It was finally
withdrawn by
CIÉ in 1962.

Not all the dramatic viaducts were on the main line. This wonderful photograph, taken in
the 1880s, shows a train on the narrow gauge system crossing the viaduct at Ballydehob,
County Cork, at low tide. The viaduct crosses the upper reaches of Roaringwater Bay.
(National Library of Ireland)

> *. . . in a piece of waste ground at or near the junction of new Mallow and old Cork and Dublin roads in the townland of Kilbarry, in the parish of St Anne's, Shandon.*

Dargan decided on a set of temporary wooden buildings for a station at Blackpool, in order to make his deadline.

The achievement of laying a line from Dublin to Cork was celebrated on 18 October 1849, when Lord Clarendon again ventured southwards, 'having acceded to the wishes of the Directors to open the line'. As the *Illustrated London News* recounted:

> *His Lordship left the Castle of Dublin at nine o'clock, and reached the Mallow station at three where the officials connected with the Cork end of the line awaited His Excellency's arrival. He shortly after started for Cork, leaving the carriage from time to time to inspect the different works of interest along the line and reached Cork at past five.*

The widespread hunger and starvation in the area caused unease among the local police and military charged with Clarendon's safety. They had also to contend with the press of minor nobility eager to make the acquaintance of the influential visitor from the Castle:

> *At the Cork station, the Earl of Bandon's dress carriage, with outriders and postillions in their state livery, awaited the arrival of his Excellency, who upon alighting from his saloon, and having been saluted with military honours, entered the carriage and was driven through the principal streets to the Imperial Hotel. Here his Lordship was entertained by the directors of the company and met, not the traders or merchants of the city, but a few of the private friends of the officials.*

A waspish comment in the *Illustrated London News* stated that:

> *It is to be regretted that some more liberal arrangements were not made with the railway directors, so as to have brought his Lordship more in contact with the citizens.*

The 'minor loyal interests of Cork' vented their resentment at not being invited to the reception in the *Cork Reporter*:

> *The mode in which the invitations for the dinner were distributed seems to have deeply offended the local shareholders, a meeting of whom is called to consider the subject.*

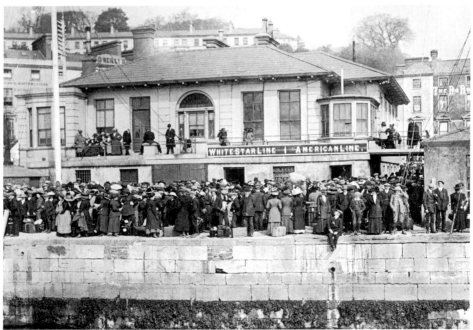

The transatlantic port of Queenstown, or Cobh, just outside Cork, was the last sight of Ireland for millions of emigrants in the post-Famine period. (National Library of Ireland) The railways delivered them in large numbers to the quayside. (Fr Browne S.J. Collection)

(National Library of Ireland)

The GS&WR connected to many of the narrow gauge systems in Munster which were built with government encouragement in the late nineteenth century. These included the famous West Clare Railway, whose station at Kilkee is shown above. County Kerry also boasted Ireland's only monorail, the Lartigue which connected Listowel to Ballybunnion (right).

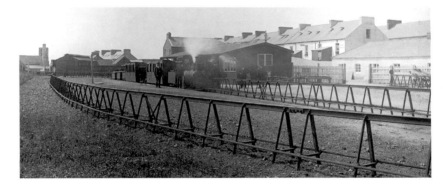

(National Library of Ireland)

It was a minor upset in an otherwise successful ceremony. The GS&WR had arrived in Cork, had received the approval of the government whose subsidies it had prudently spent and whose Lord Lieutenant in Ireland it had safely transported in the 'salubrious' saloon carriage. There would be substantial compensation for shareholders who were upset by being left out of the Cork ceremony, as the line prospered in the coming years and their heirs became the beneficiaries of the solid stock of the GS&WR.

The Midland Great Western Railway—
Cattle to Markets

F ollowing the opening of the Liverpool & Manchester Railway a great wave of railway speculation swept over Britain. Schemes competed with each other and for the public's money; railway mania was in full swing. The government could do little to regulate the situation but determined to stop the same chaos being repeated in Ireland, where railway promotion had not yet reached such a frenzied state.

In October 1836, with just the Dublin & Kingstown Railway line operating and a further two schemes—the Ulster Railway and the Dublin & Drogheda Railway—sanctioned by parliament, a Royal Commission was set up to plan a railway network for Ireland. The aim of the commission was to lay down routes which would give maximum benefit to the country at a cost which Ireland could sustain. The immediate effect was to put a halt to railway speculation until the report of the commission was released.

The Royal Commission spent nearly two years collecting evidence before its final report was published in July 1838. This report was a monumental survey of economic conditions in pre-Famine Ireland which has become a valuable resource for historians of the period. Though many eminent railway engineers were consulted, as a blueprint for a national railway system it was a failure. Even its proposal for a national gauge of 6 ft 2 inches was not adopted, except by the unfortunate Ulster Railway, who had to regauge their line when it became clear that they were the only company acting on the commission's recommendation. The commissioners proposed that Ireland's railways should be built with public money, which was never forthcoming. They were generally pessimistic about the prospect of railways being remunerative in Ireland and thus their proposed system

The Royal Canal basin in Phibsboro, from an early nineteenth-century engraving by Brocas. The fledgling MGWR purchased the Royal Canal Company and ran trains parallel to the canal for most of the way to Mullingar. (National Library of Ireland)

The Broadstone terminus of the MGWR in Dublin photographed around the turn of the century. Built to a pleasing Egyptian style, it was the work of the Midland's architect, J. S. Mulvany. Distant from the city centre at that time and never connected to Dublin's municipal tramway system, it lost its passenger trains in 1937 to Westland Row. (National Library of Ireland)

Locomotive number 27 BEE
was built in England and
delivered for the opening of the
Athlone–Galway extension in
1851. This machine remained
in service until 1897.

George Hemans,
who was Chief
Engineer with
the Midland
Great Western
Railway from
1846 to 1853.
Hemans devised
a system of
laying sleepers
and track to
take 8-ton laden
locomotive
(above) across
midland bogs.

was a modest one. They suggested a pair of main trunk lines linking Dublin with the south-west and the north-west, with branches off these serving other centres.

One of the most controversial parts of their proposals was the omission of any line from Dublin to the west coast. It was felt that the two existing canals were sufficient to cope with any traffic between those parts of Ireland. The Grand Canal from Dublin to the Shannon, built in the late eighteenth century at a substantial cost to the public purse, and its slightly later and somewhat unnecessary competitor the Royal Canal, again mainly funded with government money, were certainly not over-burdened with traffic at the time.

As it became obvious that the report of the Royal Commission was not going to be acted on, railway promotion got under way again in Ireland. As we have seen, in 1842 the GS&WR discussed a scheme linking Dublin with the west coast. When the board decided against it, a number of members left and began, in the spring of 1844, the formation of a separate company which was to build this line, the Midland Great Western Railway. The breakaway faction was led by James Perry, Quaker and entrepreneur.

The MGWR's main line was to run from Dublin to Athlone, with Galway, on the west coast, the ultimate aim. A branch was to run from a junction at Mullingar to Longford. At an early stage, in an inspired move, the fledgling company decided to purchase the Royal Canal. It acquired the stock of the canal company at a bargain price, paying £40 for every £100 of canal company stock. The track was to be laid on the level land beside the cut, which came with the purchase of the canal. The railway runs parallel to the canal virtually all the way from Dublin to Mullingar, as today's passengers on trains running from Dublin to Sligo can observe.

However, no sooner was the MGWR prospectus published than a rival scheme emerged, the Irish Great Western Railway, which had close links with the GS&WR. The GS&WR seemed to have belatedly found merit in a route to the west. Initially it was planned that the IGWR line to Athlone and Galway would leave the GS&WR Dublin to Cork line at Sallins. This was later changed to a junction at Portarlington, which meant that IGWR trains and traffic would pass along the GS&WR main line for a much longer distance, greatly increasing that company's revenues from the western traffic.

In July 1845 parliament approved a Bill for the MGWR line from Dublin to Mullingar with a branch to Longford, whilst the IGWR line was thrown out. The failure of this GS&WR-backed scheme signalled hostile relations between the two companies as they jostled for territory and traffic in the midlands of Ireland. The MGWR received parliamentary authorisation in separate Acts passed in 1846 and 1847 for extensions to its main line to Athlone and Galway. Ultimately the company would operate a main line, over 120 miles long, running through the very heart of Ireland, and from east coast to west coast.

Construction began with due ceremony at Broadstone in Dublin on 12 January 1846. The first sod was cut by the Lord Lieutenant before an 'assemblage of fashionable society' who then retired with the directors to the offices of the Royal Canal Company for the sumptuous banquet that was 'de rigueur' for such events in the last century. The works could scarcely have begun at a less auspicious time, as the full effects of the failure of the previous year's potato crop, the first act in the catastrophe which was to go down in history as the Great Famine, were becoming manifest. One positive effect of the construction of the line was to provide work for men who might otherwise have been destitute. In November 1847, 1,900 men were engaged on the works between Dublin and Mullingar. Most of the population lived on a gruel of nettles, kale, corn and bad potatoes.

In marked contrast to the directors gorging themselves after the cutting of the first sod, and much more typical of those terrible times, is a story recounted by Shepherd in his magnificent history of the MGWR. An inquest was held in Mullingar in March 1847 following the death of Michael Kelly, a labourer employed in the construction of the railway. He had come with his wife and five children from County Offaly some months previously to find work on the railway. As a result of bad weather he had had little work since the turn of the year. It was reported that he had a little gruel on the Sunday, worked all day on the Monday and died in his sleep on the Monday night. At the post mortem it was reported that his stomach and intestines were 'perfectly empty', and he had the appearance of a man who had not had food for a length of time.

Construction of the first stretch of line from Dublin to Enfield proceeded rapidly, and the directors were able to make a trial run there early in May 1847. The first section opened for traffic on the twenty-eighth of the following month, offering a service of four trains each way with connections from Enfield to Mullingar and Longford being provided by canal boats.

The railway opened as far as Mullingar on 2 October 1848. The company had by now decided to concentrate its efforts on the line to Galway. (The branch to Longford, which had been authorised in the company's original Act of 1845, was not in fact completed until 1855, long after the Galway line had been opened.) The MGWR were assisted in their objective of reaching Galway by a government loan of £500,000 towards the cost of the works, to provide some relief to the distressed districts of the west. In 1849 the contract for the whole line from Mullingar to Galway was awarded to William Dargan. Whilst construction of the line as far as Mullingar had been relatively straightforward, the extension to

On the hoof . . .
A major source of
traffic for the
MGWR was cattle,
shown here being
traded at the fair
in Spiddal in
County Galway.
The MGWR linked
the west coast to
Dublin. (Bord
Fáilte)

The principal engine shed of the Midland Great Western system at Broadstone in Dublin is
pictured here in the 1950s near the end of steam operations. (R.S. Carpenter Photos)

A cattle fair filling the main street in Belleek, County Fermanagh, in 1918. Similar fairs held in towns and villages throughout the west of Ireland sold cattle to Britain via the MGWR. (National Library of Ireland)

A goods train climbing through Liffey Junction on the former MGWR outside Broadstone in the 1950s. The rake of vehicles on the left consists mostly of cattle wagons; this traffic was still very important to the railways in the 1950s. (R.S. Carpenter Photos)

Galway involved several major engineering works, most notably the substantial bridge over the Shannon at Athlone.

The cast iron supports of the bridge were designed and built in Limerick, floated up the Shannon on barges and sunk into the clay of the river bed by a method novel for the time—the use of compressed air. When these 'hollow legs', measuring 210 feet in diameter, were ballasted with masonry, the purchase in the river bed was more than secure enough to support a length of 600 feet from buttress to buttress. The swing bridge at the centre to allow navigation underneath was also novel, sufficient to inspire a writer from the *Westmeath Independent* to describe the entire bridge as 'a beautiful and permanent piece of Art'.

The testing and loadbearing was conducted by Board of Trade inspectors observing a locomotive and train of wagons weighing 200 tons cross slowly over the central span 'without causing the slightest deflection'. This historic crossing of the Shannon, however, produced no fanfare of bands and civic joy in Athlone. There had been agitation over the sale of houses for demolition to the railway company; there had been funerals of local men killed on the stretches from Mullingar, with an inquest registering blame upon the late hours men worked. There had been strikes by masons over wages, who were seeking 18 shillings a week—about twice the rate Dargan had paid at the start of his railway building seventeen years previously.

Most of all, the progress of the railway was identified with a ruling class who seemed unable to stem famine, though they might alleviate it with employment. As the maiden voyage of the first train to cross the Shannon bridgehead continued on to Ballinasloe, Lord Clancarty entertained the directors of the MGWR in that town. Some received gifts of bullets, coins and salvages of sieges from the Williamite wars which had raged across the Shannon a hundred and fifty years before and which had been found in the excavation work on the line.

Dargan completed the works by July 1851 and the great east–west railway link opened on 1 August 1851 with an initial service of three through trains in each direction.

Once the Galway line had opened, attention turned to plans for other extensions. There had been several schemes mooted for a line to Cavan. The MGWR were interested as part of a through route from Belfast to the west coast, where several places had been proposed as possible locations for a new deep-water port for American traffic. The prospect of a great new super-port somewhere on the west coast was a vision of 'El Dorado' which lured a number of Irish railway promoters in the nineteenth century. The idea was that mail and passengers from America would land in Ireland and be speeded by train from the west coast to a port on the east, where the short sea voyage to Britain would complete their journey much faster than the ship would have taken to sail to Liverpool or Plymouth.

Various locations were mooted for such a port, ranging from Valentia in County Kerry to Clew Bay in County Mayo. Like so many grand designs, nothing ever came of it. As ships got bigger and faster, the amount of time which would be saved by a stop at a port on the west coast of Ireland diminished. The closest it came to reality was towards the end of the century, when Atlantic steamers anchored for a few hours in Cork Harbour. Irish passengers and mail were transferred by tenders coming out from Queenstown. Most famously, this was the last port of call for the ill-fated *Titanic* in April 1912.

A number of rival schemes were floated to link Cavan to Dublin or Drogheda, but when these fell apart the MGWR announced in 1852 that they intended to proceed with their Longford branch and build a route to Cavan branching off this line. Once again Dargan won the contract. Trains ran to Longford at the end of 1855 and to Cavan in July of the following year. Cavan was later linked to the north by a line running south from Clones which opened in the early 1860s. This ended on a junction with the MGWR line, providing one of the relatively rare examples in Ireland of a station shared by two companies.

Whilst the MGWR was generally on good terms with its northern neighbours, the same could not be said about its relationship with the imperious GS&WR. The MGWR had been born out of a dispute in the GS&WR boardroom and the 1850s saw the two companies at loggerheads and in constant conflict. Railway companies in the nineteenth century were very territorial, warding off those who might be tempted to build competing lines and thus affect their revenue. The GS&WR had never quite got over their loss of the west of Ireland and belatedly attempted to get a share of the traffic emanating from there. In 1854 they opened a line from Portarlington, on their Dublin to Cork main line, northwards to Tullamore. The MGWR then made an offer to purchase the Grand Canal, which ran deep into GS&WR territory. Outright purchase was resisted by their rival but the MGWR still managed to lease the canal. At this point in its history the company controlled more miles of canal than railway!

The rivalry between the two companies was costly. The MGWR offered through tickets from Limerick to Dublin. Passengers were conveyed as far as Athlone on steamers which the company put in service on the Shannon, and onwards from there by train. Passenger fares and the rates charged for the carriage of goods dropped, which was excellent for the customer but ultimately damaging to the companies, especially the MGWR, which was weaker than the GS&WR.

An early engraving (below) showing the Shannon Viaduct at Athlone, the major engineering feature of the MGWR extension to Galway. (National Library of Ireland)

A later view of the same bridge (above) taken around the turn of the century. The man standing on the left pier marks the spot which the MGWR's steamers on the Shannon used as a berth. (Mac Cormac Studios, Athlone)

The mill town of Athlone was a major junction on the Midland Great Western Railway, where the lines to Mayo diverged from the main line to Galway. (Mac Cormac Studios, Athlone)

A passenger boat on the Shannon near Athlone. As part of its war with the Great Southern
& Western Railway in the 1850s, the MGWR advertised through fares between Limerick and
Dublin via Athlone. The MGWR operated steamers on the Shannon to which passengers
were transferred at Athlone. The cost of a first-class ticket between Dublin and Limerick by
this circuitous route worked out at less than a penny per mile, but the journey could take
more than a full day. (Mac Cormac Studios, Athlone)

The GS&WR retaliated by backing schemes to extend its own line from Tullamore to Athlone and from there on to Sligo and into Mayo. The GS&WR line from Tullamore to Athlone, the route followed by today's express trains from Dublin to Galway and Mayo, was opened in 1859, but the MGWR managed to stall for nearly a year before putting in a junction between the two companies' lines at Athlone. The threat to its territory from GS&WR-backed schemes forced the MGWR to promote lines to serve these areas. An Act to extend the existing line from Longford to Sligo was passed in 1857 and, again to ward off the intrusion of GS&WR satellites, the MGWR backed the nominally independent Great Northern & Western Railway, authorising it, in 1857, to build a line from Athlone to Roscommon and Castlerea. Eventually this route was extended to Claremorris and Castlebar in 1862, Westport in 1866 and Ballina in 1873.

The disputes between the two companies were finally resolved with the help of outside arbitration in 1860. The warring parties agreed to define their territories and not to encroach on the other's patch. The MGWR were to have a free rein from Dublin to Athlone and north of the Shannon, the GS&WR would confine its activities to the south of this line.

Having resolved its problems with the GS&WR, and with its railway mileage at last in excess of its waterways, the MGWR completed its system during the remaining decades of the century. This was done both by constructing lines of its own and also by absorbing smaller companies whose lines adjoined its tracks. One of these was the Dublin & Meath Railway, whose line to Navan left the MGWR's main line at Clonsilla, seven miles to the west of Dublin. A branch off this line from Kilmessan, south of Navan, served Athboy. The D&MR route was later extended to Kingscourt in County Cavan. The section between Kingscourt and Navan is still in use today for transporting gypsum.

From Enfield a branch was opened to Edenderry in 1877. The construction of this line was made possible through the good offices of a local landowner, a Miss Nesbitt, who put £10,000 of her own money into the scheme. To honour her generosity, the point between Enfield and Moyvalley, where the branch met the MGWR line, was called Nesbitt Junction!

A short branch was opened off the Cavan line in 1886 to serve Killeshandra. The grandly named Sligo & Ballaghaderreen Junction Railway built the only branch off the Sligo line in 1874 to the small market town of Ballaghaderreen, some ten miles distant from Kilfee Junction on the main line. This remote stretch of track, which closed in 1963, became in its final years a place of pilgrimage for railway enthusiasts, as it was one of the last lines in the whole of the CIÉ network which was regularly worked by steam locomotives.

Two further short MGWR branches are worth a brief mention. Various Acts of Parliament were passed from the 1870s onwards to encourage the construction of railways in the more remote parts of Ireland. These lines were called light railways and the legislative strictures concerning their working were relaxed, as it was recognised that speeds on these lines would not be great and that the rigorous standards which were imposed on main lines need not be applied. One such piece of legislation was the Tramways Act of 1883, which is recognised as being responsible for the growth of narrow gauge railways in Ireland. However, two standard gauge lines built under its scope were both worked by the MGWR.

The first of these was the Loughrea & Attymon Light Railway, which left the MGWR's line to Galway at Attymon Junction near Athenry. The line opened in 1890 and when it closed to all traffic in 1975 it was the last country branch line left in the whole of Ireland. Once it was common on most of the main lines for express trains to stop at places like Attymon Junction, where passengers would leave the express and change to the little branch train on the adjacent platform to make the connection to a town or village in the hinterland. From Attymon Junction the branch train, often conveying goods wagons in addition to its one or two passenger carriages, would ramble through pleasant countryside, serving the one intermediate station of Dunsandle on the way, to reach the town of Loughrea some nine miles distant. The other light railway which fed onto the MGWR main lines was the twelve-mile branch from Claremorris to Ballinrobe. Built by the Ballinrobe & Claremorris Light Railway, this line opened in 1892 and lasted until 1960.

The final two routes which completed the MGWR system were the most spectacular, though the least remunerative parts of the company's route mileage, which totalled—at the time of its amalgamation in 1925 with the other railways in the Free State to form the Great Southern Railways—some 538 miles. Reference has already been made to legislation passed to encourage the building of railways in the more remote parts of Ireland. The Tramways Act of 1883 had allowed the baronies, the main unit of local government before county councils were established in 1898, to guarantee interest on the capital used to construct a line through their area. This transformed the situation for potential investors in such schemes. A very risky investment in some remote part of Ireland became a virtual meal ticket as, come what may, the interest on their capital would be paid out of the local rates from the districts it served—even if the line itself did not generate enough profit to cover the interest. It may be surmised that this was not always such a good deal for the ratepayers. The light railways to Loughrea and Ballinrobe were financed with the help of these baronial guarantees.

A passenger train at Ballaghaderreen in County Roscommon in the early 1960s. This was the only branch line off the MGWR route to Sligo and had the distinction of being among the last lines in the Irish Republic to see the use of steam locomotives on its trains.

The railway line to Galway was opened in July 1851. This view of the terminus (and hotel) dates from 1854. The Great Southern Hotel still dominates the south-eastern corner of Eyre Square.

The last decade of the nineteenth century was marked by intense political agitation in Ireland for Home Rule. Partly in response to this, and possibly in a belated attempt to assuage their guilt for the Famine, unionist politicians in Britain began to develop a more benign policy towards Ireland and its manifest problems. For unionists, as opposed to home rulers, there was the aspiration that Ireland could be brought up to the economic standards of the rest of the United Kingdom.

The British politician most commonly associated with this policy was Arthur Balfour, Chief Secretary for Ireland from 1887 to 1891. His greatest achievement was the Land Purchase Act of 1891, which, with later amendments made under the tenure of his brother Gerald who followed him in the job of Chief Secretary from 1895 to 1900, transformed rural Ireland into a land of peasant proprietors, later to become small farmers, whose produce was to be freighted on the railways. Among Arthur Balfour's other achievements was the establishment in 1891 of the Congested Districts Board, which was charged with the improvement of the so-called congested districts, an area stretching along most of the west coast from Cork in the south to Donegal in the north. The board built harbours and roads and encouraged the use of modern methods of agriculture. The need to improve what we would call today the 'infrastructure' of these areas generated other legislation in this period which further encouraged the building of railways in districts where normal commercial considerations would have dictated against their construction.

The Light Railways (Ireland) Act of 1889, sometimes referred to as the Balfour Act, was very much a product of these times. It allowed the Treasury to make direct grants for the construction of railways in economically disadvantaged areas. Out of a commission to establish where these funds could best be spent came two MGWR lines, from Galway to Clifden and from Westport to Achill.

The MGWR had already decided to build a line from Westport to Mallaranny before a visit of Arthur Balfour in 1890. He encouraged the extension of the line to Achill, with the government providing the funding. The 27-mile branch cost nearly £170,000 to construct. It opened as far as Mallaranny in July 1894 and services began over the final eight miles to Achill in the following year.

A macabre coincidence linked the first and one of the last trains on the Achill line. In June 1894 a boat carrying a large number of islanders had left Achill for Westport, to join a steamer for Glasgow (many people from Achill travelled every year to Scotland to work at the potato harvest). The boat capsized near Westport and 30 of its passengers were drowned. Though the line was not officially open, a special train was arranged to take the bodies back to the island. In 1937, just before the line closed, ten young people from Achill died in a fire at their lodgings on a farm in Scotland, where they were working during the potato harvest.

Some were related to the victims of the 1894 disaster. A special train was once again organised to bring the bodies home.

Whether such lines achieved very much in terms of economic development is open to debate, but it is surely significant that both those first and last funeral trains on the Achill branch, over 40 years apart, conveyed the remains of seasonal migrant workers. If the railway had been the force for the economic improvement of the west of Ireland that had been envisaged in the nineteenth century, then surely there would have been no need for Achill islanders to migrate to Scotland for work in the 1930s, as they had done in the 1890s.

The other line which the MGWR added to its system and which was built with government money provided under the Balfour Act was the 48-mile route from Galway to Clifden. The Treasury awarded the MGWR a grant of £264,000 to build the line from Galway through the heart of Connemara to Clifden. Work started in 1891 and the first train serving the public finally reached Clifden on 1 July 1895. Trains leaving Galway for Clifden had to reverse out of the station and then cross the Corrib on a long viaduct which was the major engineering work on the Clifden line. This had three spans of 150 ft each, and a shorter span of 21 ft which could be raised to allow waterborne traffic to pass under it. In order to promote tourism the line served the hotel built by the MGWR at Recess, twelve miles from Clifden. This opened at around the same time as another railway hotel was opened at Mallaranny on the Achill line. The final government grant to the MGWR funded an eight-mile extension of the Ballina branch to Killala which opened in 1893.

Though built with the best of intentions, the MGWR's 'Balfour Lines' were very vulnerable. There was never enough local traffic to make them pay. It had been argued that, if there was a means to take fish landed on the west coast to the markets in the east and in Britain, the fishing industry would flourish. With the coming of the railway, fresh fish could be transported across Ireland in a matter of hours, yet fishing never developed into a major industry. Nor could the seasonal tourist trade sustain a railway for twelve months of the year. In an early effort to cut costs, a petrol-engined railcar was tried on the Achill line from 1911 for a few years. However, this experiment was not pursued.

As long as the railway had a virtual monopoly of the meagre business on offer, it could just about break even. However, during the First World War the internal combustion engine rose to prominence because of its military applications. After the war, army surplus vehicles flooded onto the market at very cheap prices. These cars, lorries and buses, running at first in a totally unregulated manner, began to eat into the railway's traffic returns.

The northern end of Eyre Square in Galway, showing some of the horse trolleys which ran to Salthill. (National Library of Ireland)

The line to Clifden, which opened in December 1892, was built with government money in an attempt to open up the 'congested districts' in that part of Connemara. It was one of the early closures of the Midland system. Services from Galway ended in April 1935.

Though the promoters of the railways in the nineteenth century had hoped that Galway might have been developed as a port for transatlantic traffic, in the end the only regular passenger traffic to use the port were the services to the Aran Islands. (Bord Fáilte)

Lines such as these were very vulnerable to competition. Whilst the branch to Ballina is still very much in business, the Killala extension closed to all traffic in 1934. Railway services to Clifden ended the following year. As we have noted, the Achill branch succumbed in 1937.

At its peak, the MGWR was Ireland's third largest railway. It bestrode the middle of Ireland with virtually no competition from other companies. If you wanted to travel from Westport or Mullingar to Dublin, you had no alternative to its trains. The service of passenger trains provided by the company, whilst adequate, was never lavish. In 1897 there were four through trains each day to Galway. The first and last trains of the day, leaving Dublin at 7.00 in the morning and at 8.20 in the evening, were known as the Limited Mail and the Night Mail respectively. As their names implied, they carried mail as well as passengers. The morning mail train arrived in Galway at 10.51 a.m. Contracts with the post office to deliver mail were an important part of every railway company's revenue. The running of these trains was strictly regulated by the postal authorities and their timekeeping was closely monitored. In the days when the written word and the postal packet were the primary means whereby people kept in touch with each other, and the most important way of conducting business, getting the mail trains through on time was of paramount importance.

The 1897 timetable showed that Sligo was served by three trains out of Dublin, in addition to a train from Mullingar which formed a connection with the morning Limited Mail. This arrived in Sligo at 11.03 a.m. Most branch lines had two or three passenger trains a day, in addition to a daily goods train. The MGWR did its best to promote tourist traffic on its western lines. From 1903 to 1906 a special train known as the Tourist Express was put on, leaving Dublin at midday and arriving at Clifden at 5.00 p.m. This train had its carriages painted in a special livery and included a dining car, a relative rarity in Ireland at the time. It is interesting to note that the number of trains in today's timetable to Sligo, Galway and Westport is much the same as at the turn of the century.

One type of traffic which contributed a considerable amount to the revenue of the MGWR was livestock. The railway passed through countryside which was well suited to the raising of sheep and cattle. In 1891 it was reported that, out of a total of 5,580 goods trains run by the company, 1,723 were livestock specials. These carried 853,018 head of livestock from 1,150 fairs. The biggest of all the fairs was held at Ballinasloe in October each year, described by one observer as the biggest gathering of sheep and cattle in the British Isles. In 1881, for example, this fair created enough business to fill 446 wagons, which were dispatched by twelve special trains.

It was the Englishman's love of his roast beef that paid the dividends of many shareholders in Irish railway companies. Cattle reared and fattened on the lush green pastures of the midlands were either sent to Dublin to market, from where they were driven through the streets from Smithfield to the docks, or taken directly to the steamers by the MGWR's connecting line to the North Wall. As late as the 1960s long trains of cattle wagons trundled along the former MGWR lines bound for England, though by that time the locomotives which hauled them were modern diesels and not steam engines of MGWR vintage. Between 1922 and 1924 the MGWR added a new class of 23 large and handsome six-wheeled goods engines to its fleet. Though they were equipped for use on passenger trains as well as for freight traffic, the railway's staff always referred to them as the 'cattle engines'. The railway was aware, from the boardroom down to the most menial factotum, of the importance of livestock traffic.

Mention of the cattle engines leads us on to a brief look at the sort of steam locomotives which hauled MGWR trains throughout the company's independent years, from the 1840s to 1925. Some of the very first machines were made by Thomas Grendon & Company of Drogheda. They supplied five locomotives in 1847 and one of these, *Dunsandle*, hauled the opening train. As the century progressed and trains got heavier, the MGWR, like most of the main railway companies, settled on six coupled tender locomotives for its goods and cattle trains and four coupled engines for passenger services. The company did not possess many tank engines, as suburban traffic into its Dublin terminus never really developed, unlike some of the other lines which served Ireland's capital.

Most MGWR locomotives had names which were a mixture of poetry and eccentricity. Some bore the names of the places they served, like *Maynooth*, *Clara*, *Lough Corrib* and *Clifden*. As was common in the early years of the railways, names from classical mythology were also used, such as *Hercules*, *Cyclops*, *Sirius* and *Orion*. Three machines dating from 1878 were called *Hibernia*, *Cambria* and *Caledonia*; *Britannia* did not come until a year later. There were some odd ones as well, like *Wolf Dog*, *Ouzel*, *Bat* and *Titanic*—which retained her unfortunate name even after the disaster of 1912.

Like all the railway companies located wholly within the Irish Free State, the MGWR became part of the newly-formed Great Southern Railways in 1925. The dominant force in the new company was the MGWR's old rival, the GS&WR. Changes gradually took place. Locomotives lost their names and were painted grey. The MGWR station at Broadstone in Phibsboro in Dublin was closed in 1937 and Midland line services were transferred to Westland Row. It has to be said that The Broadstone was never convenient for the city centre and it also lacked a tramway connection. The handsome office building and entrance to the station, built in the Colonial Egyptian style, is used now by Bus Éireann. The train shed behind the façade, from whence the Tourist Express and the Night Mail for the west used to depart, has been altered over the years in its new role as a bus maintenance depot, but its railway origins are still apparent.

With the exception of the lines to Achill, Clifden and Killala, which closed in the 1930s, most of the former MGWR system survived into the CIÉ era, though it was decimated by the closures of the 1950s and 1960s. Today only trains to Sligo take the MGWR line, alongside the Royal Canal. Part of the old main line, from Mullingar to Athlone, whilst still in existence is no longer used by regular services. All trains for Galway, Westport and Ballina leave Dublin's Heuston station and branch off the Cork line at Portarlington, reaching Athlone and former MGWR tracks via Tullamore. This represents the final triumph of the grandees of Kingsbridge over their upstart breakaway colleagues at Broadstone, who had the nerve to part company with the GS&WR in the 1840s in order to bring railways to the west of Ireland.

CHAPTER FIVE

Irish Railways 1900–1952— Growth and Decline

The years from the turn of the century until the eve of the First World War are often referred to as the golden age of the railways. This was as true in Ireland as elsewhere in Europe. It was claimed that no inhabited part of Ireland was more than ten miles from a railway. The national railway network was nearing its zenith. The number of route miles of railway topped the 3,000 mark in 1894 and peaked at just over 3,400 in 1920. By the 1890s the main trunk routes were completed, as were most of the cross-country lines and the branches which fed into both. Aided by government legislation and Treasury money, some of the last gaps in the system were filled, including the MGWR lines to Achill and Clifden (mentioned in Chapter Four) and many of the narrow gauge lines, which were seen as the salvation of remote communities in the north and west of the country.

Notable among the Irish narrow gauge railways was the Letterkenny & Burtonport Extension Railway, which enabled the trains of the Londonderry & Lough Swilly Railway to reach the tiny fishing port of Burtonport on the north-west coast of Donegal, a line which would never have been built without the £300,000 from the public purse that was spent on it. The Burtonport line opened in 1903 and two years later a pair of the most powerful steam locomotives ever to run on the narrow gauge were put to work there. More powerful than many locomotives running on the broad gauge at the time, the Lough Swilly 4-8-0 tender locomotives were more than a match for the steep gradients of the new line.

Despite the power of these locomotives, it still took at least five hours to cover the 74 miles from Derry to Burtonport. Allegedly to keep the jarveys in business,

True steam. A train of the Waterford, Limerick & Western Railway in one of the bay platforms at Limerick Junction. The WL&WR was taken over by the Great Southern & Western Railway in 1900.

many of the line's stations were miles from the villages they were supposed to serve. Where an experienced traveller saw the word 'Road' in the name of the station he was heading for—such as Dunfanaghy Road on this line—his heart must have sunk, for it usually meant the station was miles from his destination.

Most of the lines built in the first decades of the twentieth century were short-lived, none more so than the line from Armagh to Castleblayney, which opened in 1910. In a strange way this line harked back to the great debate of the 1840s as to whether the main line from Dublin to Belfast should follow the coastal route or an inland one. The Castleblayney, Keady & Armagh Railway was the last link in the inland route. It was never used for through trains between Ireland's two major cities and closed a mere thirteen years after it opened, although the section from Armagh to Keady lingered on for goods traffic until the 1950s.

One other line dating from this period which is still in use is the one from Rosslare to Waterford. Opened in 1906 by the Fishguard & Rosslare Railways & Harbours Company to provide a link from the developing port of Rosslare through to Cork via Waterford, this was a significant late addition to the railway network. Today this line through the south of County Wexford still sees a sparse service of passenger trains, but it is especially busy in the late autumn conveying sugar beet from Wellington Bridge to the sugar factory at Mallow. Since the closure of the direct line via Dungarvan in 1967, these trains take the scenic route via Limerick Junction.

During the First World War Ireland's railways were taken into government control under the aegis of the Irish Railways Executive Committee (IREC), which was charged with regulating all aspects of railway activity. The First World War was a conflict in which railways played a major role across Europe. In August 1914 the plans of the great powers for mass mobilisation of their armies were heavily dependent on the railways. Failure of diplomacy may have been the main cause of the conflict but it is not fanciful to say that the inexorable and unbending logic of railway timetables across Europe made war inevitable once the orders to mobilise had gone out.

In Ireland the government committee set rates and regulated train services to maximise the contribution the railways could make to the war economy. The government determined to maximise production in Ireland's meagre coalfields to reduce the country's dependence on coal imports from Britain at a time when every ton of coal produced there was needed for the war effort. The IREC arranged for the building of several new railways to serve coalmines in various parts of the country. A ten-mile branch was opened from Athy to the collieries at Wolfhill in County Laois in 1918. Not far away another line was built branching off the Portlaoise to Waterford route north of Kilkenny to serve Deerpark colliery at Castlecomer, though this did not open until 1920, too late to help the war effort. A final legacy of the committee was the extension of the Arigna branch of the Cavan & Leitrim narrow gauge line to serve the coalmines in the Arigna valley. This line had been proposed and fought about almost from the commencement of services on the C&L in 1887. The Arigna Valley Railway, which opened in 1920, and the coal trains which passed over it, were the main reason for the survival of the C&L until 1959, by which time it was one of the last remnants of 500 miles of 3 ft gauge tracks which were once such a feature of the railway network.

Among the places seized during the 1916 Rising, and one of the last to surrender, was the Westland Row station of the Dublin & South Eastern Railway. The Rising was mainly confined to the Dublin area and there was relatively little disruption to the railways. The commander of the Volunteers at Westland Row, Eamon de Valera, was to be responsible for much more damage to the Irish railway network as Taoiseach in the 1950s than he was in 1916.

The railways were put under some pressure during the War of Independence, although damage to them was relatively limited. In some instances drivers refused to take out trains conveying British soldiers or munitions, and some sections of line, mostly in the west, were periodically closed.

One memorable incident occurred on the County Donegal Railways. The general manager, Henry Forbes, was a feisty character whose political views would not, to say the least, have been in sympathy with those opposed to the Union. In September 1920 he was a passenger on a train on the CDR branch from Donegal to Ballyshannon which was stopped by armed raiders at Drumbar, a few miles from Donegal Town. Seeing the train crew held at gunpoint he slipped quietly out of his carriage and onto the ballast and made his way to the engine. He then exchanged shots with the would-be train robbers, who fled. Forbes managed to capture one who tripped over in the course of his flight. He was led captive back to the train and escorted under the armed guard of the general manager—one might say railroaded—back to Stranorlar, where he was handed over to the police.

The War of Independence was followed by the Civil War, which was triggered by the rejection of the Anglo-Irish Treaty by dissident republicans. During this conflict the railways in the newly established Irish Free State suffered destruction and disruption of a severity not endured before nor since. In certain parts of the country trains were regularly derailed or robbed. One of the worst affected was the Dublin & South Eastern Railway, which had the misfortune to serve the counties of Wicklow and Wexford, where anti-Treaty forces were well organised.

One of the most spectacular crashes on an Irish railway occurred at Harcourt Street station in Dublin in 1900. A cattle train from Wexford ran out of control and the locomotive crashed through the buffer stops at the end of the platform. Although the crew were injured and a great amount of damage was done, the locomotive was soon back on the rails. As a consequence of the accident the Board of Trade stipulated that all trains had to stop at Ranelagh before proceeding to the terminus.

Last of their breed. Locomotives ready for duty outside the running shed at Inchicore in the 1950s not long before the advent of the diesels.

U class 4-4-0, number 204, bearing the GNR's beautiful sky-blue livery, passes non-stop through Enniskillen in the early 1950s. Ireland had relatively few 'named' trains over the decades. One of the best known was the Bundoran Express, which ran to the County Donegal seaside resort, where the Great Northern Railway had their own hotel. The train ran non-stop from Dundalk through to Pettigo. Because it did not stop in Northern Ireland it was not subjected to customs examinations, as most trains on the cross-border lines were at that time.

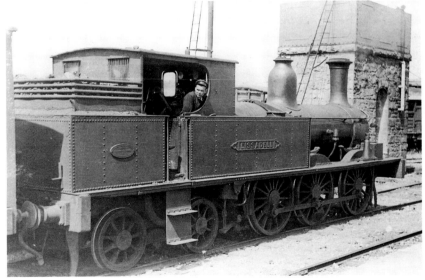

0-6-4 tank locomotive Lissadell, named after the home of one of the directors of the line at Manorhamilton. The last independent standard gauge railway in Ireland was the Sligo, Leitrim & Northern Counties Line, which ran from Enniskillen to Sligo. This line, which depended heavily on cattle traffic, was unusual in that its fleet of locomotives never carried numbers, only names.

Between July 1922 and April 1923 over fifty attacks were made on this system. Nearly twenty signal cabins were destroyed—the majority by arson—bridges were blown up and trains were attacked and robbed or set on fire. One of the most destructive incidents on the D&SER occurred on 23 January 1923 at Macmine Junction in County Wexford, where a branch to New Ross and Waterford left the main Dublin to Wexford line. Raiders took over the station and arranged a malicious triple collision and fire which completely destroyed one locomotive and three carriages and caused serious damage to other rolling stock.

The lines of the GS&WR were also heavily attacked. The single most disruptive incident of the whole period was the explosion which in 1922 destroyed the central span of the viaduct which took the Dublin to Cork main line over the River Blackwater at Mallow. A temporary station called Mallow South was opened whilst the viaduct was being rebuilt; passengers and goods had to be taken by road from there to Mallow from where they could continue their journey. The original structure had been made of stone. Its replacement, which consisted of steel trestles built upon the footings of the original piers, is still intact, a legacy of those turbulent times, when W. T. Cosgrave asserted the right of the fledgling state to run its railways by travelling in the locomotive that made the journey over the repaired Mallow Viaduct.

During the First World War, with the railways under government control, many changes had taken place. With traffic probably doubling in these years, government control had led, as in Britain, to a rise in labour costs due to increases in wages and the onerous hours which railway staff worked. In 1919 the Irish Railways Executive Committee imposed an eight-hour working day on the reluctant railway companies, bringing to an end a situation which had pertained since the beginnings of the railways, under which staff were often expected to work very long hours. The conditions of employment for railway workers had long been of concern to the inspectors of the Board of Trade, whose job it was to regulate the railways and investigate the causes of accidents. Numerous accident inquiries had cited the length of time the staff involved had been on duty as a contributory factor to accidents.

The problem for the railway companies was that they had to employ more people to do the same amount of work, and this added greatly to their wages bill. During the war, arrears of maintenance accumulated, with little money being put aside for renewal of track and rolling stock. Whilst the railways were compensated by the government after the war—the largest of the companies, the GS&WR, getting over three-quarters of a million pounds—the wartime legacy of inflated labour and coal costs, and the lack of money for investment in track and rolling stock, put the railways in a very vulnerable position, at a time when the internal combustion engine was coming into its own.

The disruption of the Civil War put a further strain on the railways and, for those in the Free State at least, the future looked bleak. Amalgamations and take-overs had occurred since the beginning of the railway age. The GS&WR had grown to its great size largely by taking over smaller companies for a fraction of what it had cost to build their lines. In 1901, in one of its biggest acquisitions, the GS&WR had absorbed the Waterford, Limerick & Western Railway, whose tracks extended from Waterford to Sligo. The process continued in 1922, when the Cork, Bandon & South Coast Railway amalgamated with the GS&WR.

For years a variety of interests had been urging that Ireland's railways should either be nationalised or made to amalgamate into one large company. The new government of the Irish Free State was receptive and in 1923 decreed that if voluntary amalgamation between the companies could not be achieved then the government would legislate. The Dublin & South Eastern Railway held out, but from 1 January 1925 it became part of the new company which was to run all the railways—the Great Southern Railways. The GSR took over all the companies whose lines were located wholly within the twenty-six counties.

The years of revolution had led to the creation of two states in Ireland with an international border between them. Straddling that border was the Great Northern Railway, itself the product of an earlier amalgamation in 1876 of a number of northern companies. Apart from its Belfast to Dublin main line, the GNR had long cross-country lines running from Dundalk on the east coast to Bundoran on the Atlantic shores of County Donegal. GNR tracks crossed the newly-established border in seventeen places. All the lines which crossed the border were excluded from the GSR and, along with those which operated wholly within Northern Ireland, remained independent. Apart from the GNR, such unassuming routes as the Sligo, Leitrim & Northern Counties Railway, running from Sligo to Enniskillen, the Londonderry & Lough Swilly, based in Derry—though almost all of its tracks were in Donegal—and the CDR now found themselves operating across an international frontier.

There was a humorous side to this, such as excursion trains to Bundoran in the month of December during the Second World War, run for the benefit of smugglers rather than bathers at that time of the year, and two sets of bar tariffs in the dining cars on the Dublin to Belfast express, the price of a drink depending on which side of the border you were when served. But the reality for the cross-border railways was one of disruption and expense, which arguably hastened the demise of many of these routes. Passengers and their luggage were subjected to searches

Compound GNR 4-4-0, number 84—Eagle—has the right of way at Great Victoria Street station in Belfast with an express bound for Dublin in 1937. The rebuilding of the Boyne Viaduct in the early 1930s meant that the Great Northern Railway could use these heavier locomotives on main-line services. (Rail Archive Stephenson)

In 1939 the GSR produced the first of three of the largest locomotives to run in Ireland. The 800 class, named after deities in the ancient Celtic pantheon, were designed as the Dublin–Cork expresses. They were so heavy that they were restricted to the Cork main line. Bedevilled by coal shortages during and after the wars, these magnificent machines had little chance to show what they could achieve before the coming of the diesels made them redundant for main-line services in the mid-1950s. Near the end of her days, the first of the locomotives, number 800—Meadhbh—is seen at Dublin's Kingsbridge station. This locomotive may be viewed at the Ulster Folk & Transport Museum's Railway Gallery at Cultra in County Down.

A locomotive passes through the disused Bessbrook station with the train for Dublin, near the end of steam working on the Great Northern Railway main line in the 1960s. Present-day Newry station is located at this point on the GNR main line. (Des Fitzgerald)

Typical of the many country junction stations which were scattered around the railway network is this one at Ballyhaise, on the GNR line from Clones to Cavan. A train to serve the branch to Belturbet waits for the connecting service from Clones to arrive. (The late Gerry Douglas, courtesy of Chris Banks)

at border crossings by customs officers with limited social skills. Apart from petty inconveniences, the real problem with the border was that it was drawn for reasons of politics, by sectarian head counts, and economic considerations played no part in it. Most railways were built to serve established trade routes. The promoters of the UR back in the 1830s were interested in a railway to Armagh, and beyond, where the trade was, rather than an undoubtedly more prestigious line to Dublin. Those companies now found themselves faced with a political settlement which disrupted established trading patterns.

Perhaps the clearest example was the case of the Londonderry & Lough Swilly Railway Company and the city of Derry. Part of the city's natural economic hinterland was the Inishowen Peninsula and north-west Donegal, and the L&LSR was the railway which served this district. All but the first four of the system's one hundred or so miles of narrow gauge track were now in the Free State, yet the workshops and head offices were in Northern Ireland. The districts served by the L&LSR were far from being prosperous at the best of times. Now different duties and tariffs on either side of the border disrupted and delayed trade at a time when road vehicles were eating away at the railway's traffic. By the late 1920s the L&LSR was in trouble. The line from Buncrana to Carndonagh closed in 1935 and the epic route to Burtonport was scheduled to close completely in 1940, though wartime shortages of fuel for replacement road vehicles gave a stay of execution until 1947. The Swilly's answer was to become a road transport undertaking and in this form it survived. In its new role the growing fleet of Swilly buses and lorries were subjected to different legislative regimes on either side of the border: even the maximum speed at which its buses were allowed to travel was different.

The reality of independence in the south did not quite live up to the billing. These were bleak and barren times. The haemorrhage of emigration continued unabated. The new state was inward looking, asserting its own identity by expressing its differences from its powerful neighbour across the Irish Sea. When de Valera came to power in 1932 a row with Britain over the non-payment of land annuities escalated into the so-called economic war. Both sides imposed punitive tariffs on each other's exports. This was much more damaging for Éire, as the United Kingdom was by far its biggest market. The value of the country's vital agricultural exports fell from nearly £36 million in 1929 to £13.5 million in 1935.

When a country's economy is performing poorly, railways suffer. The Great Southern Railways reflected the state of the nation in the retrenchments and closures which it undertook between 1924 and 1945. It also unwittingly reflected the times in the choice of livery for its steam locomotives—a depressing shade of grey. Only 59 steam locomotives were put in service by the GSR and 26 of these had already been ordered by the MGWR before the formation of the new company. In 1934 and 1935 the GSR went mad and built a total of ten 0-6-0 goods engines. Their design was supposed to improve on the old GS&WR 101 class of engines, which dated back to the 1860s and were by far the most numerous of any steam locomotive design in Ireland. These new engines serve well as a metaphor for their builders, as this attempt to improve on a tried and tested 60-year-old design was deemed to have produced a machine which was greatly inferior to the one it was intended to update.

In fairness to the GSR, it was faced with a multitude of problems. It took over a national network of railways which were in poor shape. The damage caused by the Civil War had to be addressed at a time when competition from buses and lorries was reducing revenue. Legislation in 1924 abolished the system of baronial guarantees which had encouraged the promotion of railways in remoter parts of the country in the last thirty years of the nineteenth century. Under these guarantees the ratepayers of a district underwrote interest on capital and any working losses of these lines. The compensation given to the GSR by the state for continuing to work these lines was inadequate. The worldwide depression which followed the Wall Street Crash in 1929 and the economic war with Britain added to the company's difficulties. There was little money for capital investment at a time when much was needed. Lines which had been built late in the nineteenth century were in need of renewal by the 1930s as both track and rolling stock reached the end of their useful lives. Lack of money meant that the GSR had to soldier on with outdated equipment. This made the railways of Ireland a joy for nostalgic railway buffs but a nightmare for those who had to run the trains.

The GSR's answer to this situation was retrenchment. Many miles of double track were singled, notably long stretches of the former MGWR main line to Galway. Closures became inevitable. Among the early casualties were the two narrow gauge lines serving Cork city, those run before the amalgamation of the Cork & Muskerry and the Cork, Blackrock & Passage companies. Broad gauge branch lines began to succumb, the one to Kinsale in 1934 and the former MGWR lines to Clifden and Achill in 1935 and 1937 respectively. Other branch lines lost their passenger services at this time. More would have closed but for the onset of the Second World War, when a severe shortage of oil for road vehicles gave many lines a reprieve.

If amalgamation was to be the answer to the railway's problems in the south, the new Northern Ireland state did little to change the status quo. The GNR and the other companies whose lines crossed the border carried on as they

At its peak there were over 500 miles of 3 ft or narrow gauge railways throughout Ireland, usually built in the more remote parts of the country where a full-sized line might not have been a paying proposition. At Strabane in County Tyrone a goods train bound for Donegal town prepares to leave the station. (Keith Christie)

The Cavan & Leitrim narrow gauge system survived until 1959. The main reason for its continuing existence was the fact that the branch from Ballinamore to Arigna, which ran alongside the public road for much of the way, served one of Ireland's few workable coal deposits. Here a train of Arigna coal is rattling along the tramway hauled by one of the line's original 4-4-0 tank locomotives which dated from the 1880s. (Colin Hogg)

The Londonderry & Lough Swilly
Railway was one of the largest
operators of narrow gauge lines in
Ireland, with 99 route miles of track.
Parts of the system were abandoned
as early as the 1930s. The Swilly
began to operate buses instead of
trains and several of their buses are
seen on the opposite platform. By
1953 only the lines from Derry to
Letterkenny and Buncrana remained
open for goods traffic. 4-6-0 tank
locomotive number 3 stands at
Letterkenny station with the goods
train from Derry. The L&LSR is still
in existence as a bus company.
Going back to 1853, this is surely
one of the longest-lasting transport
undertakings in these islands.
(John Edgington)

A Dublin–Cork express in the early 1950s, seen near Rathpeakin. It comprises
eight coaches and two post office vans, hauled by J15 class 0-6-0 number 104,
dating back to the 1880s, and B2 class 4-6-0 number 401.

had before, as did those companies whose tracks were located entirely within the new state. These ranged from the busy Belfast & County Down to the tiny Castlederg & Victoria Bridge Tramway. The one significant change was brought about by events in Britain, where the independent companies were forced to amalgamate by the government in 1923 to form four large companies, rather in the style of the GSR.

The English Midland Railway had significant interests in Ulster following their acquisition in 1903 of Ireland's fourth largest company, the Belfast & Northern Counties, and their joint purchase, with the GNR, of the County Donegal narrow gauge system in 1906. In 1923 the MR, including their Irish lines, became part of the newly formed London, Midland & Scottish Railway. Managed by the Northern Counties Committee based in Belfast and backed by the resources of one of the biggest railway companies in the world, in marked contrast to the railways in the rest of Ireland, these lines did have much needed investment. The 1930s saw them operating their main lines to Derry and Portrush with some of the fastest steam-hauled expresses ever to run in Ireland.

The railways in the north suffered two major setbacks in the 1930s. The first was a damaging and bitter strike in 1933 which was provoked by pay cuts imposed by the managements. The GNR suffered two malicious derailments during the strike, and the NCC narrow gauge line from Ballymena to Larne lost its passenger services. The benevolence of the LMS had provided this line in 1928 with a set of the finest coaches ever to run on the Irish narrow gauge, for use on boat trains connecting with the steamers to Scotland at Larne Harbour. They had electric lighting, steam heating, lavatories and corridor connections, luxuries undreamed of elsewhere on Irish 3 ft gauge line.

The second setback was a direct result of legislation passed by the Stormont government. With the flood of cheap vehicles coming onto the market after the First World War, a large number of small local bus operators became active throughout Ulster. The BCDR and the NCC had been running buses and lorries for many years to connect with their trains and provide cartage services from their goods depots, but following legislation in 1927 the railway companies bought out many of these independent operators and co-ordinated their road and rail interests in what would be described today as an integrated transport system.

At this point the Stormont government decided to bring all public service road transport, passenger and freight, into the hands of one company. An Act was passed in July 1935 creating the Northern Ireland Road Transport Board. Railway companies in Ulster could no longer run road vehicles. NIRTB lorries and buses, often based on railway property, were supposed to work in co-operation with the railways and provide feeder services, but in fact competed with the railways for both passenger and freight traffic.

As the war clouds were gathering over Europe in 1939, there emerged from Inchicore works in Dublin the first of a trio of steam locomotives which were the largest and most powerful to run in Ireland. They were numbered 800 to 802, and named *Meadhbh* (Maeve), *Macha* and *Tailte* after deities in the Celtic pantheon. They were also the most powerful locomotives of the 4-6-0 wheel arrangement seen in Europe. Painted green, not grey, they were so heavy that they were restricted to the Dublin to Cork main line, where they were to work the most important expresses. No sooner were the 800s in service than supplies of coal imported from Britain virtually dried up. Britain had little coal to spare for the neutral Free State.

At the same time petrol for private road vehicles became scarce. Traffic lost to the roads in the years since the formation of the state, both passenger and goods, poured back onto the railways. Because of the shortage of coal, services had to be drastically cut, especially from 1942 onwards, to conserve what little coal was available. Alternatives such as peat were tried with limited success. Irish mined coal, which was generally of poor quality, was unsuitable for use in the engines.

Trains were withdrawn from many branch lines, some for as long as three years. In other cases, like the lines from Woodenbridge Junction to Shillelagh in County Wicklow and from Birdhill to Killaloe in County Clare, both of which were closed 'temporarily' in 1944, services were never restored. The coal shortages in the south continued after the war, and over ninety steam locomotives were converted to burn oil in an attempt to improve the situation. Normal services were not fully restored until the end of the 1940s and it was a tragedy for the magnificent 800 class locomotives that they had scarcely time to show what they could do on the Cork main line with decent coal in their tenders before the arrival of diesel locomotives in large numbers from 1955 onwards.

The GSR, the one-time 'premier' line, was criticised for poor services and high fares. The continual loss of traffic and the company's poor financial performance were such that by 1938 liabilities were exceeding income. In that year the government appointed a commission to report on ways forward for the company. This commission recommended nationalisation, but in the meantime the government had assumed control of the GSR for the duration of the Emergency.

Meanwhile, up in the north there was plenty of coal for the railways as part of the war effort. As in the Free State, petrol was severely rationed, which brought more traffic back to the network. Northern Ireland played a significant role in the

S class 4-4-0 number 171—Slieve Gullion—prepares to leave Derry with the passenger train in the early 1960s. The closure of this line in 1965 by the Ulster Transport Authority deprived the counties of Tyrone and Donegal of their last rail links. Happily, number 171 still survives in the care of the Railway Preservation Society of Ireland and has been used since the 1960s on special trains throughout the country. (Craig Robb)

In the 1950s the most modern steam fleet in Ireland was that which operated on the lines of the former Northern Counties Committee in Northern Ireland. Most of their locomotives had been designed and built by their affluent English parent, the London, Midland & Scottish Railway. Here W class Mogul, number 91—The Bush—leaves Belfast York Road station with a train for Derry. (H.C. Casserley)

*A Great Northern
Railway P class 4-4-0
locomotive dating from
the 1890s near Fintona
Junction in County
Tyrone with a train from
Omagh to Enniskillen.
These elderly Victorian
locomotives steamed out
their last days on the
GNR line between
Omagh, Enniskillen
and Dundalk which
was swept away in
the railway closures
of 1957.
(A.D. Hutchinson)*

*Ranelagh station on the Harcourt Street line to Bray shortly before closure in 1959. Of all
the closures of the 1950s and 1960s, that of the route from Harcourt Street in Dublin to
Bray caused little controversy at the time but much later. The millennium will see a new
light rail system, LUAS, operating on the tracks of the old route. (Michael Costeloe)*

A railcar on the County Donegal narrow gauge system. One of the reasons the County Donegal narrow gauge lasted until 1959 was that from the 1930s onwards it was a pioneer of diesel traction. Railcars were built which stopped at level crossings as well as stations along the system, providing an economical passenger service to the remote communities that the railway served. (John Langford)

production of Allied munitions, warships and aeroplanes. Agricultural production was also stepped up to compensate for unobtainable imported food. The railways were heavily used by the armed forces. Ulster's airfields and dockyards were vital in protecting the North Atlantic shipping routes. New airfields were built and existing ones extended. At RAF Ballykelly in County Derry the extended runway crossed the rail line from Belfast to Derry, and special arrangements were made linking adjoining signalboxes with the airfield's control tower to prevent trains 'meeting' aircraft of the Coastal Command on the runway.

Following the entry of America into the war thousands of GIs poured into Ulster to prepare for the invasion of Europe, and the soldiers and their supplies all had to be moved around by train. The province also suffered from the attention of the *Luftwaffe*. The worst air raid on Belfast occurred on Easter Tuesday 1941, killing 740 people and injuring over 1,500. Among the many targets hit, destruction was wrought on the Northern Counties (NCC) station and yards at York Road.

The impact of the war on the traffic returns of the railways on both sides of the border can be judged from some GNR statistics. GNR, of course, operated in both jurisdictions. The 5,000,000 passengers carried in 1939 had risen to 11,000,000 in 1944. Around 1,000,000 tons of goods traffic was handled in 1939 and this had risen to 1,750,000 tons by 1944. The GNR's turnover virtually trebled and holders of ordinary shares saw their first dividends for many years.

It was, of course, too good to last. Once the oil began to flow again and the cars, buses and lorries were back in business, traffic deserted the railways as quickly as it had come back to them during the war. Soon the wartime bonanza for the railway was over.

The post-war government of Northern Ireland followed much the same course in relation to its railways as did Dublin. The Stormont parliament passed legislation setting up the publicly-owned Ulster Transport Authority from 1 October 1948. The UTA took over the NCC, BCDR and the NIRTB. The only nominally independent railways remaining in Ireland, apart from the GNR, were the remains of the L&LSR system, the CDR and the Sligo, Leitrim & Northern Counties Railway. Reaction was bitter among railway enthusiasts.

As one railway historian has noted of the UTA:

> *The fact that this ignoble cabal survived for twenty years proves conclusively that there is no God or if there is one He goes round by bus.*

He continues:

> *The Ulster Transport Authority had a profound anti-railway bias from the day it was set up. By 1950 it had closed down all of the BCDR except the branch to Bangor. In its inglorious career, in cahoots with the government of Northern Ireland, it wiped out most of the railways in Ulster, with the exception of lines from Belfast to Bangor, Larne, Portrush, Derry and Dublin (at one point they even proposed reducing this main line between Ireland's two largest cities to a single track). The UTA left a gaping hole covering most of the province of Ulster on today's railway map of Ireland.*

The GNR's short-lived prosperity of the 1940s resulted in the company investing in a new fleet of diesel railcars in 1948 and some additional steam locomotives, including the five VS class 4-4-0s built in 1948 for the main line. These engines, named after rivers in GNR territory, in the company's beautiful sky-blue livery, were among the most handsome machines to grace an Irish railway.

Whilst revenue held up reasonably well, operating expenses soared and from 1949 onwards the GNR was making heavy losses. In 1950 the GNR board announced that they could no longer continue as a private company and threatened to close the whole system. In an act of cross-border co-operation unusual for the time, the parliaments in Dublin and Belfast passed legislation acquiring the company. A statutory body, the Great Northern Railway Board, was set up, with its members appointed in equal numbers by both governments. This body kept the spirit and ethos of the Great Northern alive until 1958, when it was abolished and the remains of this great undertaking were nationalised and absorbed into CIÉ in the south and the Ulster Transport Authority in the north.

From the Republic to the Millennium—A Tale of Revival

By the end of the Second World War, the state of the railways mirrored that of the country—contracted and without clear direction. The policy of neutrality, though rooted in a need to demonstrate political independence from Britain, had cost the south much in terms of material supplies and psychological isolation. While a victorious Britain and a shattered Europe set about rebuilding, isolated Ireland limped along on an economic shoe-string, unaided by the massive injections of American capital which were among the fruits of Allied victory. Though neutrality had strengthened confidence in self-government, it had the downside of depriving the country of the technical advances of the war effort and the emotional momentum of building a country 'fit for heroes to live in', which had been Lloyd George's promise to revitalise Britain after the First World War.

'A railway hardly fit for humans' was the recurring criticism. Fuel shortages and the need for major investment to refurbish the network confronted the government with the necessity to do something positive and radical. Having suffered Dáil defeat on a previous move to take the railways into state ownership, the returned Fianna Fáil government, in June 1944, set about buying out the stockholders and forming a unified national transport company which would run the rail, bus and haulage services as one organisation.

Modelled along the lines of the 'semi-state' companies which had successfully harnessed the latent potential of bogs for fuel (Bord na Móna) and rivers for electricity (Electricity Supply Board), the new company would be called Córas Iompair Éireann, or Transport Authority of Ireland. It would take into its control most of the railway lines in the Free State and be charged with a dual remit to provide a

**RAILWAYS OF IRELAND
IN 1947**

Lines open for traffic as at 1st January 1947

———— **STANDARD BROAD GAUGE**
- - - - - **NARROW GAUGE**

*The railway map of Ireland in 1947 showed relatively few changes from the system at its greatest extent
in the 1920s, though some branch lines and several narrow gauge routes had been closed by this time.*

The fate of the Irish narrow gauge is best summed up by this picture of the remains of the Owencara Viaduct in north Donegal. A train was blown off the viaduct in 1925 by gales coming in from the Atlantic. A large amount of government money was sunk into building this line at the turn of the century. By 1947 it had been abandoned. (Jonathon Christopher)

The Great Northern Railway terminus at Foyle Road in Derry was built in a style not dissimilar to that of Amiens Street in Dublin. After the line closed in the 1960s, this delightful Italianate structure was bulldozed out of existence. (Derek Young)

satisfactory public service while becoming economically viable. Córas Iompair Éireann soon became known as CIÉ, achieving populist recognition via widespread 'branding' of rail carriages with a logo which the wits christened 'the flying snail'.

The new body had been formed with political rancour. A government motion to amalgamate the various lines in May 1944 had been defeated following an acrimonious debate which heard allegations of corrupt share-dealing in the stock of the GSR, whose shares had escalated in value in anticipation of such a move. Taoiseach de Valera had resigned, driving to Phoenix Park at midnight to inform the President, occasioning risible comment in the satirical magazine *Dublin Opinion*, which used the railway as a metaphor for his political manoeuvring. Opponents alleged that de Valera had deviously used Dáil defeat on the railway Bill to seek a fresh electoral mandate.

He was returned with an increased majority, sufficient to pass much pressing legislation other than that of the creation of CIÉ, which came into being on the first day of January 1945.

CIÉ inherited a potentially formidable but sprawling and disparate inventory of land, stations, main lines, branch lines and canals, rolling stock and employees. Under the umbrella of the new authority came 2,000 miles of railway track, thousands of pieces of rolling stock for freight (ranging from the barely functional to the antique), 500 locomotives (many of which were older than the century), 600 omnibuses, 600 road haulage vehicles, 300 horses for goods delivery in cities, and the Inchicore railway works which manufactured locomotives and carriages.

In effect, CIÉ was taking into its care, and hoping to integrate, a century of piecemeal railway evolution of large and small companies, and main and branch lines (standard and narrow gauge), as well as the ancillary ownership of hundreds of houses, commercial hotels, canals, rights of way and freight depots. In human terms, CIÉ was now responsible for 20,000 employees, making it the largest private employer in the state. A job on the railway, whether clerical or manual, was secure and pensionable employment at a time when such security was much sought after in a depressed economy with high emigration. Since the beginning of the century a job on the railway meant something, especially in rural areas, where a house often came with the status of station-master, driver or gate-keeper. Inchicore works in Dublin was one of the few instances of a 'heavy industry' manufacturing in the state. It provided expertise in machine-tooling and heavy metal working, without which the rail network could not have functioned.

The Inchicore works were just outside Kingsbridge station on the line to Cork. 'The Works', as it was known locally, was a powerhouse of light and heavy engineering, making everything from brass fittings and carriage interiors to the legendary giant locomotives *Meadhbh*, *Tailte* and *Macha*. During the 1940s The Works was still an expression of the industrial revolution which had given it iron life. Paddy McElroy, later to become a sculptor in metalwork, started his working life there as an apprentice in the wagon shops. Like most at The Works he had a family connection with the railways, and started there at sixteen in 1939. He recalls that, after probation, he earned 10s a week:

> *I gave 7s 6d to the Mammy, which was expected, and had 2s 6d a week for myself, which was riches then. As an apprentice blacksmith I had menial tasks to begin—holding the red hot iron in tongs for the blacksmiths to shape—the Smithies were big men, walked with a certain swagger and would only talk to other Smithies. The Works was a place of heat, sweat, strength and skill. Roaring furnaces, smoke, iron clanging on iron—and by contrast there were little corners where men were engaged in delicate tool-making. You could have roaring furnaces at one end where wheels were cast before being taken to the machine shop for finishing at the other end.*
>
> *There was a hierarchy of skills and nicknames. 'The Lancer Lynch' and 'Bugler Dunn' owed their names to being in a mounted regiment in the Boer War, and a particular shed was known as 'The Khyber Pass' because some of the men there survived that 'skirmish'. Then the jobs had nicknames—'Smoke Box Charlie' cleaned out part of the engine, 'the trimmers' laid the fires, and the job of a 'knocker-upper' was to go around the railway cottages and wake up the engine firemen in the early hours.*
>
> *Many of the men had seen service in two or three wars; some had been with Dublin regiments in the Boer War, then in the 1914–18 war and some again in the Civil War. So there were often tensions to do with politics. Some parts of The Works were known as nationalist and were rumoured to have made clandestine weapons for 1916. Certainly The Works made munitions for the Great War, brass shells and the like. And in the Civil War the armoured locomotives made in Inchicore put paid to some of the republican attacks on the railways.*
>
> *And yet on Armistice Day when I was there it was a matter of local pride for those living in the railway cottages to come out and cheer the men who marched with their arrays of ribbons and medals. You could be working alongside a man who had seen active service and not know it unless you were told. On Sunday the foremen dressed in their suits and bowler hats and had watch-chains and went to Mass or to the Baptist churches, of which there were a number from the days when The Works were set up by skilled tradesmen from England who came over to Dublin.*

Some attempts were made to modernise the railways in the 1960s, the most obvious being the demise of the steam locomotive and its replacement by modern diesel trains. Cosmetic alterations were made to stations. Many travellers will remember the 1960s makeover at the former GNR terminus at Amiens Street.

Commuters boarding a southbound train at Westland Row. Before the DART, suburban services on the coastal line were provided by diesel railcars.

More efficient ways of handling goods were introduced on the railways in the 1960s and 1970s. One innovation was the conveyance of fertiliser in special wagons which could take pallets. Here a train of the specially built wagons is being loaded at the Nítrigin Éireann plant at Arklow.

New air-conditioned coaches were gradually introduced from the 1970s. An A class locomotive, number 001, hauls coaches on a scenic part of the run between Dublin and Wexford.

'Management' and 'work practices' reflected more the custom and service of the end of the previous century than the volatile change that the rest of Europe was undergoing in the wake of the war. The 'bosses' of the railway were invariably Protestant and upper middle class, tracing their privileged position to the nineteenth-century origins of the railways. The headquarters offices of the principal lines were modelled on the offices of colonial administration in London's Whitehall, with sweeping marble staircases that led to brass-plated doors, more resonant of a District Commissioner than of a District Engineer. Within that imperial system, the culture of railway working had evolved into a patriarchy, whereby sons took over from fathers or were recommended by relatives—a job culture that was a century in the making by the 1940s. This was not confined to the managerial class but percolated throughout the entire railway network, creating an artisan community which set railwaymen and their families apart from other trades and professions, in a similar way to the army and the police force.

Indeed, the army seemed to provide the model for this system, with the officer class of the railway being composed of engineers and clerical workers who sat regular examinations for promotion. On the physical side of the railway work, the foot soldiers were the gangers and plate-layers, who could expect a lifetime of labouring work maintaining the permanent way, while the drivers of the locomotives underwent at least six or seven years' apprenticeship as engine firemen, to which rank they graduated from engine cleaner. As with other trades and professions, a family tradition counted, even at the most basic level of skill. Growing up in Athlone in the 1930s, Eamon Lacken inherited this strict hierarchy. His grandfather had worked on the remote Killala road in County Mayo (railwaymen often referred to the line as 'road') and had been given a railway cottage on moving to Athlone, where his son, in turn, would become a fireman and get a railway house on his marriage. Growing up in that railway tradition, at the age of fourteen Lacken was given a three-minute interview with the Shed Foreman, who was busy marshalling locomotives. 'He told me if I came in at half past eight on Monday morning I would get "the start".' Lacken began as a 'temporary apprentice engine cleaner' in October 1939. The railways were to be his life:

With my father's overalls I arrived as a fresh-faced cleaner and was presented with a scraper and told to scrape the wheels of a steam engine, and I can tell you it was a very bleak, cold kind of job after leaving the comfort of school. But at the end of the week when you got your 25s and there was 1s 3d stopped for a stamp, you forgot the misery of the week, with this wonderful pound in your hand, and gave it to your mother and held on to 3s 6d to enjoy yourself for the next week.

During the war years Lacken saw the service deteriorate as coal imports from Britain declined. Turf, wood and improvised mixtures of coke and slack were substituted, extending train times from Dublin to Athlone from two-and-a-half hours 'that you could set your watch by' to five and sometimes seven hours. He recalls that one journey of about 40 miles took 17 hours on poor fuel, which included burning cardboard. Experiments were made mixing tar, cement and sand to replace coal, but 'nothing could beat good English coal from Yorkshire', for which the engines were made.

By the end of the war Lacken had become a fireman, which meant constantly shovelling coal from the tender to keep the fire-box at the optimum temperature needed to drive the engine, which could be as heavy as eighty tons, and to pull the laden carriages. On a 130-mile journey from Galway to Dublin he shovelled between two and three tons of coal into the fire-box, single-handedly. In the hundred years' evolution of locomotive technology, the principle was still the same—traction power by the pressure of steam, generated by burning coal.

In spite of the hardships of travelling by rail at that time, the routes were busy. Apart from passengers on the straight line to the west, the railway was also heavily used for the export of 'dry stock' cattle from the central breeding plains. The viability of the MGWR, which built the lines to the west (see Chapter Four), cannot be divorced from the voluminous growth of cattle exports to Liverpool and Birkenhead from the Irish midlands. A century of rail access had induced midlands farmers to concentrate on cattle breeding for export. Immediately after the war years, as CIÉ was consolidating, cattle were still a principal source of freight revenue. At the height of the export season, freight trucks were converted into rough living accommodation for drovers to sleep, overnight on the long haul to and from the east coast.

A drover of that time remembers that a coal-burning stove was constructed in the middle of the truck, with the chimney sticking out of the roof. Coke and wet 'slack' were snaffled from railway yards to keep the drovers warm as they slept in rough wooden bunks on the night journeys from Dublin to the cattle fairs of the west. Billy-cans were heated on the stove for breakfast. On arrival, the cattle were loaded and they began the long haul back again, with interchanges made to bring them onto the quayside at Dublin, where the cattle were driven onto the boats at the North Wall, bound for Birkenhead.

By 1948 a number of changes had impacted upon the railways. The Free State had become a republic, leading to an increased awareness of being responsible for its own affairs. But the railways were in continual decline, mirroring the contraction of the country's economy. Revenue was not helped by

A goods train on the Great Northern main line near Drogheda in the late 1950s. The arrival of the A and C class diesels in the period 1955/57 revolutionised the railways of CIÉ and banished much-loved steam locomotives. (J.G. Dewing)

The changeover from steam to diesel is portrayed in this view of a diesel railcar and a WT class tank locomotive at Whitehead station in County Antrim in the mid 1960s. The WT class were the last steam locomotives to see active service in Ireland, a few lasting into the early 1970s. (Craig Robb)

the growing usage of motor cars and buses, or by continuing emigration. Yet the railways provided a crucial service to the fragile economy, such as the constant ferrying of fuel to midland turf stations and the movement of massive amounts of beet to the sugar factories—by 1956 the system would carry 1.9 million tons of beet. Railways also continued to facilitate the stable agricultural economy, transporting 'live cattle' from all regions of the country and delivering them to the North Wall at Dublin, where the rail lines converged, and onto the boats for export to England.

The antiquated railway system was losing about £1m a year during the 1950s, yet proposals from the management to cut staff numbers and branch lines met with government resistance. A government which agreed severe cuts in regional areas would face retribution at election time. This was to become a repeated pendulum swing of debate—the railways should provide a satisfactory public service yet should also pay their way.

One future finance minister was to gain ground-level insight into that perennial debate when he joined the railway as a ticket clerk and was posted to Dromod in County Leitrim. Albert Reynolds remembers:

> It was my first permanent job—on the junction of the narrow gauge which ran from Dromod to Ballinamore and on to Ballyconnell and Belturbet. I was selling tickets to passengers and organising the distribution of goods which came into the railhead and had to be checked and dispatched for distribution by road. There was a lack of morale in the whole countryside and there was a lot of talk about CIÉ closing down. There was no investment taking place, the rolling stock was 75 or 100 years old. It wasn't a great environment to be working in, although I enjoyed the camaraderie—a job on the railway meant a lot.
>
> Although I did not realise it at the time, I learned a basic business training there—how to deal with people, balance cash at the end of the day and keep track of things. I was lucky. There was mass emigration at the time, mainly to England. I had a job, I didn't have to go, I was one of the lucky ones. It was like being in the Post Office; it was a 'permanent job'. Everyone in the locality knew you and you knew everyone, because almost everyone took the train at some time or other, until they would make the last journey—out.
>
> One afternoon a neighbour came in, a man I knew well. He arrived for a ticket to Birmingham, which was £2 10s, and he handed in £3 and I knew that was all he had; he was a bit embarrassed about it. I gave him out the ticket and I asked him did he have any more money and he said, 'No—that's my lot.' He had a brown parcel under his arm with a few bits of clothes in it. So I took back the ticket and

reached up to a shelf where there was an old stock of tickets that I knew would not be counted for a long time [in an audit] *and gave him one of those and pushed back the £2 10s and said, 'Look, the best of luck and I hope you make it.' Twenty-four years later as Minister for Finance I walked into a function in Birmingham and the first guy up to me was Mel Farrell from Roosky, who by then had a family of six, had done very well, and he said to me, 'I owe you £2 10s.' I said, 'No, you owe it to CIÉ.'*

Reynolds remembers the railways in the 1950s as 'serving the community but mainly taking their customers to the boat trains'. However, there was much else wrong with the railways, as the Milne Report of 1948 had found. The average age of the locomotives was 51 years, with high costs of maintenance and repair. Milne recommended that 100 of the 'pensioners' should go to the breaker's yard—some had run up a million miles of service since the late nineteenth century. A British railwayman with a fondness for steam, Milne resisted the CIÉ management's ambition to change the system over to diesel traction, which was the evolving technology on American and European networks. Diesel locomotives could work 18 hours a day, but Milne regarded such intense usage to be unlikely in the more limited terrain of Ireland, and therefore uneconomic.

Railway technology was reflecting wider transport changes. Air travel, for instance, was about to convert from propeller to jet. Milne resisted other management plans to drastically cut branch and narrow gauge lines and he addressed the crucial financing issue, which was to become a perennial conflict between government and railway, by suggesting ways in which the constant drain of moneys could be renamed as 'subsidies' instead of 'losses'. It would be another thirty years before government fully took on board the lesson that there was a price for demanding the *dual mandate* of 'public service' when equally demanding that the railway 'pay its way'. If the railways were required by statute to deliver home the last three passengers to a remote area, then someone had to bear the cost.

In the order of things, that contradictory demand would eventually be resolved by the one-time Dromod clerk of railway finances who had, in the intervening years, ascended the political ladder. As Transport Minister, in 1981 Albert Reynolds would promote a revised system of government financial accounting which priced 'social service' as a separate part of the railways' remit—and the state paid for it.

Back in 1949, however, another Reynolds (but no relation) had fallen foul of the testy relations between senior civil servants and railway management. Arthur Percy Reynolds had been a Lemass–Fianna Fáil appointee as chairman of CIÉ.

He had been criticised by Milne for his management decisions as well as the amount of power he held ('wrong in principle that the control of a large public undertaking should rest almost entirely upon the shoulders of a single individual'). When Milne made his report in 1948, Fianna Fáil was out of government. The succeeding Minister for Transport, Daniel Morrissey, used Milne to berate the previous administration. The merits—or otherwise—of railway reform became lost in political point-scoring. As in the Civil War, and many times since, the railways had become a pawn in political gamesmanship, which could be read as recognition of their importance as sinews of service to communities. Arthur Percy Reynolds, who had challenged many of Milne's assertions—on diesel, branch closures, plans to build Busáras in Dublin—was dismissed as head of CIÉ by his new political masters.

The rancorous fall-out further infected the already acerbic relations between railways and politicians. Too many unforeseen changes had occurred for railways to hold on to the dominant position they had enjoyed in the nineteenth century. Two wars had accelerated the design and popularity of the internal combustion engine—the motor car was becoming a widespread aspiration in a changed society where wages had increased considerably.

Unreliable trains—which were still the subject of periodic post-war shortages of imported fuel—had alienated a public that demanded better. In the cities the motor scooter became the rage of individual mobility. In one telling statistic, the number of motor cars at a race meeting in the Curragh exceeded the number of passengers taken there by several trains. Freight traffic was still mainly profitable, but the increasing number of lorries on the road was making another hole in revenue. The wage bill was huge compared to output per employee. By 1950 the railways were 'losing' the state £5,000 a day. Someone had to cry 'halt' and it fell to the coalition government, led by John A. Costello, to do so, through the aegis of Transport Minister Morrissey. This first 'inter-party government', as the coalition was popularly known, had embraced radical measures in other areas, notably the formal change from being a member of the Commonwealth to becoming a Republic. It showed similar mettle in the decision to nationalise the railways, previously the subject of much agonising.

Nationalisation—for long a bogey—in fact came in like a lamb. One day it was CIÉ, the next it was CIÉ, except now wholly owned by the Republic and legally charged 'to promote an efficient, economical, convenient and properly integrated system of public transport'. The old problem of the railways having to pay their way was still there, including government requirements that they be both 'efficient' and 'economical'. As the railway historian Mícheál Ó Riain remarked,

The changing face of
the railways related
to motive power.
One of the last
surviving traditional
GNR signal cabins,
that at Poyntzpass,
was still in service
into the 1990s.
Above, the signal box
and old-fashioned
level-crossing gates.
The gates were
opened by a wheel in
the signal box to
allow the passage of
trains. (Jonathan
Christopher)

Inside the signal cabin, levers and traditional block instruments controlled signal points and made sure that only one train was on a section of track at a time. Left, the new colour light signals are in place beside the old Great Northern semaphores—soon to be gone. The works at Poyntzpass were part of the modernisation of the Dublin–Belfast line for the new Enterprise trains in the late 1990s. (Jonathan Christopher)

'no significant voice was raised in favour of the state providing regular financial support for CIÉ'.

Although a substantial capital investment of £7m had been allocated to kick-start the 'new' CIÉ, the repeated failure to define and price the social service element would compound the difficulty of making the railways 'economical'. Half of the £7m was rapidly used up by the immediate necessity to replace rolling stock to ward off a total collapse of the network. Orders were placed for diesel railcars, so in that respect modernisation was projected. Steam was on the way out and the withdrawal and scrapping of many venerable old steam engines caused great sadness for railway enthusiasts. Yet, for all the acrimony between civil servants (charged with prudent spending of state money) and railway managers (charged with providing a public service), out in the wider reality passengers on day excursions to important national sporting occasions could get a charge of another kind—the excitement of being moved *en masse* from remote areas to Dublin for big events.

In the bleak 1950s such events were the highlight of the year for rural populations, the train journey to Dublin being an integral part of the sporting calendar. The GAA would not have flourished during that era of high unemployment and emigration without the railway, and provincial life would have been the poorer. Without the rail network, small farmers, whose produce literally provided the 'backbone of the economy', would have led even more restricted lives on meagre incomes. An account from that time of a Cork hurling follower puts the railways uniquely into context.

Many of the men in the village rose before dawn to get a lift into Mallow, in order to be in time for the first train that would get us to Dublin. Some went on bicycles, some walked. There was a fierce crush to get on the train; the corridors would be full of men standing and red-and-white flags hanging out the windows. We took sandwiches and cold tea in lemonade bottles. It was a great thing for a young fellow to go with his father and listen to the talk along the way. You heard more history and parish gossip during the five hours it took to get to Kingsbridge. Dublin was like a foreign country; I had never been there, but I remember the pride I felt as we got off the train and marched along the quays to find a place for Mass. Everyone was in good humour as we followed the crowds into Croke Park. Outside, fat women were selling oranges and chocolates. There was nervousness to see could we get in—if we had enough tickets or had to buy some from the Dublin jackeens who were selling them. Young fellows like myself were lifted over the turnstiles. I remember more about the train journey up than the match itself. It always took longer getting back, dark when we got back to Mallow. The match and the journey would be the talk of the parish for weeks afterwards. At eleven I had become an adult, because I had been on the train to Croke Park.

The railways provided that rite of passage for generations of Irish males. Such scenes of rural life were etched upon a collective memory that would also include less happy scenes of departure for the 'boat train', as the local trains were known which connected with the departure times of the boats from Dublin to Liverpool and Holyhead.

The modernisation in the operating departments of CIÉ's railways began in 1951 with the arrival of the first of a fleet of AEC-engined diesel railcars, similar to those which were put in service by the GNR in 1948. This was followed in 1953 by the issuing of a tender for the purchase of 100 diesel locomotives. The contract was won by Metropolitan Vickers and in 1955 the first of these locomotives, which were designated the A class by CIÉ, were put in service. These machines rapidly replaced steam locomotives on main-line passenger and goods services. No prototypes had been ordered and so the infrastructure to maintain such sophisticated machines was lacking. The Crossley diesel engines used for these locomotives—derived from marine engines—were very unreliable. However, most of the A class, re-engined with General Motors power plants in the 1960s, remained in service. The A class were shortly followed by their smaller sisters, the C class, which were meant for branch line and secondary routes and were also long lived. Many will recall that a number of these locomotives finished their days pushing and pulling de-engined railcars between Howth and Bray on the suburban service which preceded the introduction of the DART electric trains in the 1980s.

With overall yearly losses for CIÉ (in all areas of transport) projected to exceed £2m during the mid-1950s (£40m–£50m in today's values), an internal government memorandum concluded that 'the railways are outmoded as a form of transport, particularly in a small sparsely populated country'.

This gloomy judgement was supported by railway experience in Britain and Northern Ireland. CIÉ's own conclusion was that many branch lines were demonstrably uneconomic, if one 'balanced' running costs against revenue generated by any particular line—as the company did in the case of the Dublin–Shanganagh–Bray commuter line from Harcourt Street, which in one recent year had revenue of £21,000 against operating costs of £77,000, most of which went in wages to the 70 workers employed on the twelve-mile stretch. By 1958 the line served an upper middle-class catchment who could afford motor cars. Passenger use had diminished to about 1,000 a day.

Since the 1960s CIÉ has purchased diesel locomotives from General Motors in the United States and Canada. The 201 class, delivered in the 1990s, are the largest and most powerful diesels to run on Irish railways. Number 219 rests on the sidings at Connolly station in 1996. (Jonathan Christopher)

General Motors diesel 081 brings a train of 1960s-built Cravens coaches into Amiens Street on a suburban service from Drogheda. The electric wires for the DART trains can be seen on the left. The electrification of the Howth–Bray line was one of the significant developments on CIÉ's railways in the 1980s. (Jonathan Christopher)

In the Republic the continuing high emigration rates, in excess of 50,000 adults per year, meant that, in effect, 1,000 customers a week were leaving on a one-way ticket. But who would order the closure of the system and bear the political fallout? Dodging that likely confrontation, the government ordered yet another inquiry into the transport system.

'The Committee of Inquiry into Internal Transport' became known simply as the Beddy Report, after its chairman Dr J. P. Beddy, whose career included expertise in emigrant demographics, industrial investment and company leadership. Seán Lemass called it 'the best of the very many reports upon our transport system'—a view endorsed by historian Mícheál Ó Riain who described it as 'detailed and thoughtful'.

Beddy addressed the contentious core issue with a parliamentary kick-to-touch:

We would incline more readily towards the view that railways should be abandoned if we felt there was no possibility of radical changes being made to adapt them to the background against which they must operate . . . as now constituted and operated we see no reasonable justification for the continuance of the railway undertaking.

The qualification 'of adapting them to the background against which they must operate' allowed Beddy to make a case for rescue. Beddy projected that over half the network would be made redundant, as would 150 stations, three-quarters of the total. There would be some revenue from sale of land and property, but more substantially from a severe reduction in jobs—all costed as a financial saving. No effort was made to cost the social value of branch lines.

Significantly, CIÉ was unable to provide Beddy with a breakdown of local traffic and costs for many branch lines. As Ó Riain asked rather pointedly in his commentary, who would take the responsibility of deciding which lines would be terminated? Hardly the Dáil, the majority of whose deputies were from regional areas and 'would run scared of such a prospect'. Political considerations aside, it was widely recognised that Beddy had, in Ó Riain's phrase, 'thought through the baggage of history, controversy and prejudice' in arriving at an analysis which accurately reflected the economic realities of the rail service during the 1950s.

Beddy had addressed the haemorrhage of emigration and consequent depletion of potential rail customers, the switch to the private motor car by many rail users, and the changed transport practices of commercial companies who were increasingly using road for freight. The inability of rail management to make savings and the obduracy of trade unions stood in striking contrast to rail territories of similar size abroad. One comparison showed that—on a yardstick of a million passengers carried—CIÉ was employing three times the number of people as employed on other rail systems.

Opponents to the report queried the basis of comparison, though in defence of Beddy it was also generally, if privately, accepted that many jobs on the railway were 'false jobs'—neither unions nor politicians were prepared to publicly confront the reality that, during a decade of penal emigration, putting men out of work also meant consigning their families to temporary penury and local stigma. But even the most sentimental of returned visitors could tell there was something badly wrong with a rail system whose rolling stock was run-down and whose unkempt employees seemed slipshod in their attitudes towards passengers.

Beddy commented on the 'regrettable absence of friendly co-operation between management and unions', citing a figure of 2,000 meetings between the parties where on only one occasion was the wider culture of the railway discussed—all the other meetings were about money. At one rail and bus terminus, the unions resisted amalgamating the separate 'parcels offices' for road and rail, although neither depot required the numbers deployed. More examples left a clear impression of a system stagnating under management inertia, but, as managers bitterly asserted, they already knew much of what needed to be done— the problem was they were not allowed to act on their own judgement. Government consistently refused to sanction savings measures which would provoke the trade unions.

By the time the Dáil came to debate the issue, it had already been ventilated by newspaper editorials which accepted the necessity to drastically cut services and branch lines but warned against a high fallout of unemployment. This analysis was generally accepted by public opinion, but the logical follow-through was resisted, a characteristic of the public (and of newspaper editorials) which was of little help to a government charged with responding to the Beddy Report.

The 1958 Transport Bill displayed great ingenuity. Government would write off accumulated debt, amounting to £16.5m. (This was mainly interest on previous loans from the government to repay accumulating debt which in turn was overdue—had the government insisted on repayment 'on the nail' it could have placed the railway into immediate bankruptcy.) In addition, government would not require the company to pay a further £3m for the southern assets of the GNR (Great Northern Railways), which had already made drastic cuts in branch lines along the border. Government would pay the GNR. The railways would be given legislative freedom to become commercially competitive with road transport and to upgrade freight and passenger services. Dieselisation could continue at full pace.

When Irish railways were dieselised in the 1950s and 1960s, the operators in the North preferred railcars to locomotives, whereas CIÉ continued to use conventional locomotives hauling trains of unpowered coaches. The new diesel railcars delivered to Iarnród Éireann were the Arrows, built in Japan in the early 1990s. A two-car set leaves Amiens Street on a service to Drogheda. (Jonathan Christopher)

When Northern Ireland Railways needed new diesel locomotives for the Dublin–Belfast service in the 1980s, they too went to General Motors in the United States, who have produced every diesel locomotive running in Ireland today. The NIR Enterprise to Belfast waiting for the starting signal at Connolly station (middle). At the adjacent platform, the waiting Sligo train will be hauled by an identical locomotive in IR livery. (Jonathan Christopher)

A feature of the 1990s has been the increase of suburban traffic in and around Dublin. Regular suburban services now run to Maynooth and, on the Great Northern line, to Drogheda and Dundalk. 201 class diesel number 234 hauls a northbound service through Portmarnock station which is being reconstructed to cope with the growing number of commuters using it. (Jonathan Christopher)

135

In return for these substantial concessions, the railways would be given five years in which to break even, by which time, as the Transport Bill put it, 'operating expenditure shall not be greater than revenue'. Essentially, CIÉ would have to effect the widespread closure of 'uneconomic' lines, as outlined by Beddy. Government would fund redundancies, to within six months of the break-even period of March 1964.

The question of which lines to close would be solely 'a matter for CIÉ. As Lemass closed the debate with the intention 'to produce proposals which will be . . . workable', his words were being interpreted as the writing upon the wall of the CIÉ boardroom at Kingsbridge station. The submissions of CIÉ—whose main plank was the curtailment of competitive road traffic by law—received little attention. The *how* of solving the railway crisis had been laid down by the Beddy Report and largely endorsed by Lemass. Therefore a new *who* would take 'radical measures' to save the railways.

Among a handful of people who helped modernise post-war Ireland, Todd Andrews stood head and shoulders above his contemporaries, with a tall physical presence that was matched by his record in making two viable national industries out of tourism and bogs. By the time Lemass asked him to take charge of the railways, Andrews was deeply skilled in managing large groups of employees. Within weeks of taking charge, senior staff were left in no doubt that this particular new broom would sweep thoroughly.

Unlike many previous holders of the job, Andrews had the advantage of the confident backing of his political mentor, Lemass, with whom he shared a business-like approach to the wider remit of 'nation building'. He began by insisting that railway workers improve their general demeanour—they were to regard the public as 'customers'. Appalled at the rundown regional stations, he allocated funds for face-lifts and landscaping. Piles of rusting rails which had traditionally decorated approaches to major stations were sold for scrap and replaced by flower-beds. Onto the funeral pyre went skeletal hulks of wooden carriages which seemed to have been rotting for generations—not only a bad advertisement to the travelling public, but also, as Andrews saw it, an unwelcome metaphor for the stagnant state of the railways.

Andrews set up his own managerial network, rapidly promoting his young protégés to the newly-created rank of Area Manager. His dynamic personality ensured the revolution would be communicated widely. Improved internal communication came through staff newsletters, seminars, bonus and reward systems. Telephone replaced the telegraph for internal usage, and private secretaries gave way to typing pools. When his root-and-branch review was seen to be effective, Andrews 'topped up' with an explanatory offensive to media, politicians and business to prepare opinion for what the modern railway enthusiast may think was 'the unkindest cut of all'—the closure of many branch lines.

Some went quietly, with 'bowed head to the scaffold', according to one local bereavement ceremony. The closure of Harcourt Street merited mention in the Dublin papers, but hardly any protest other than whimpers of nostalgia for an era going . . . and gone. Dundrum and Shanganah were dairy districts on the outskirts embracing the promised land of urbanisation with the ready sale of land for housing. Looked at from today's traffic snarls on roads from South Dublin, the closure of Harcourt Street to Dundrum seems to have lacked foresight of impending growth into a commuting population which passed 100,000 by the 1980s.

Todd Andrews listed rigorous procedures being followed before closure, including 'enquiries addressed to government departments seeking information about future developments'—a claim that might bear investigation in light of the subsequent enormous urbanisation of the Dundrum district.

Other dependent communities rallied, invoking Church and State to gain reprieve. By 1961, the august de Valera, one-time promulgator of rural values in a famous speech, found himself under pressure as President to receive delegations intent on preserving the West Clare and West Cork lines, with both of which he was familiar from his seminal political activities. Now as President he was 'above politics' and could not meet them. Andrews, anyway, would not have tolerated interference with his mandate. West Clare accepted the inevitable. Cork continued to kick up a fuss, in keeping with its reputation as 'an independent Republic'. According to historian Ó Riain, after many efforts to get him to meet them, Andrews received a Cork delegation and took the wind out of their sails by asking how many of them had come to Dublin by train. Not one, apparently.

All of the once extensive network of narrow gauge lines had closed by 1961. The last to survive was the West Clare system. Once the butt of Percy French's humour in the song 'Are Ye Right There Michael Are Ye Right', this line was a byword at the turn of the century for shoddy operating practices and general incompetence. One line in the song suggested that the permanent way was so queer that the train spent most of its time off the track. Whilst this was an exaggeration on the part of the lyricist, it was indicative of the way the railway was run. In fairness to CIÉ, itself often the subject of uncomplimentary remarks, the West Clare system was completely dieselised in the 1950s, with new railcars for the passenger trains and a fleet of three diesel locomotives to operate the line's goods trains. Despite this investment, giving a part of the Irish narrow gauge system a chance to face the future with hope, the experiment failed.

The executive train in the late 1980s offers comfort and luxury in its well-appointed coaches. (Iarnród Éireann)

Architect Sancton Wood's magnificent Heuston (Kingsbridge) station, built in the 1840s as the headquarters of the Great Southern & Western Railway; as impressive today as it was 150 years ago. Until the late 1990s the magnificent edifice was separate from the train shed behind. Iarnród Éireann has modernised the station.

An artist's impression of plans for the redevelopment Connolly station, Amiens Street. The original edifice of the 1840s has been incorporated into the modernised station to meet the needs of the twenty-first century.

THE RAILWAYS OF IRELAND - 1969

Lines open for traffic as at January 1969

The closures of the 1950s and 1960s left a greatly diminished railway system. However, the lines which survive have a viable future and are attracting increasing numbers of passengers. The greatest gap ranges across the border counties. From Mullingar to Derry, a distance of about 130 miles, you will not encounter a passenger railway.

Losses mounted and the last train ran on 31 January 1961. Some of the displaced railwaymen never forgave Percy French, claiming his song had set a frame of mind among passengers which was unsympathetic to the route.

A large part of the broad gauge network was also axed. In truth, many of the lines had little chance of survival in the second half of the twentieth century—but for the war and the deficiencies in the Irish road network, a lot of the closures of the 1950s and 1960s would have happened earlier. Amongst notable losses in the south were all the lines in West Cork, those formerly owned by the Cork, Bandon & South Coast Railway, and the direct route from Cork to Waterford via Dungarvan. Most of the country's branch lines also closed. Other sections, such as the North Kerry line from Tralee to Limerick and the long meandering route from Limerick to Sligo, lost their passenger services. In many cases this was a prelude to complete closure.

Geographically, the cuts were fairly evenly spread. The border counties had already suffered the sundering of lines through Monaghan and Cavan. Neither the capital, the regions nor the coastline were spared. All of the routes owed their existence to the great railway mania of the nineteenth century which had transformed mobility by connecting hill and coastal peoples, villages to towns, towns to cities. Railway had changed remote fishing settlements into fashionable resorts. In tandem with telegraph and newspapers, whose usage the railway facilitated, these branch lines had effectively brought rural Ireland into the twentieth century. By 1959, 'not paying their way', they were regarded as having served their day.

By way of contrast, the position of the railways in Northern Ireland was a much bleaker one. The former NCC and BCDR networks were nationalised by the government of Northern Ireland in 1948 with the formation of the Ulster Transport Authority. It is doubtful if there has been a railway operator in the whole of Europe more hated or vilified than the UTA. Within a couple of years it closed all the system except the branch to Bangor. The daily traffic chaos in east Belfast is an enduring testament to this folly. Much of the NCC system followed, with only the lines to Larne, Portrush and Derry surviving into the 1960s.

The gaping hole in a railway map of Ireland of today dates from this period. You can drive the 130 or so miles north from Mullingar to Derry and not cross an operating railway on your way. From 1952 the GNR was run by a board appointed by both governments. In 1957 the government of Northern Ireland unilaterally withdrew its support for the services on the cross-border lines from Dundalk to Enniskillen and Omagh and from Portadown to Cavan. The parts of these lines which were in the Republic were useless without the connections through Northern Ireland and CIÉ had no alternative but to reluctantly go along with the closures. Among the casualties was Ireland's last remaining independent standard gauge railway, the Sligo, Leitrim & Northern Counties Railway from Enniskillen to Sligo. Without the connections eastward from the county town of Fermanagh, there was no outlet for its traffic, which consisted mostly of cattle.

Those sensing an underlying political agenda to these closures had their fears confirmed in the 1960s when the UTA insisted on closing the former GNR line from Portadown to Derry and the line to Newry and Warrenpoint. Singling of the double-track Dublin to Belfast main line in the north was also proposed. Conspiracy theories abounded at this time of a policy on the part of the Stormont government to isolate the mainly-nationalist west of the province. Whatever the reason, the once magnificent Great Northern Railway, arguably Ireland's finest railway, was reduced to its main line and one branch from Lisburn to Antrim. Today the counties of Donegal, Tyrone, Fermanagh, Monaghan, Cavan and most of Armagh, Leitrim and Down have no rail service at all, a legacy of those 'axing' days.

Happily, from the nadir in their fortunes, Ireland's railways have been on the comeback trail ever since. Against the economic upswing of the early 1960s in the Republic, something of the essential adventure and pleasure of train travel started to creep back, with improved catering and creature comforts. Marketing campaigns reflected changes in lifestyle, targeting week-day excursions for women on 'shopping specials' from the provinces to Dublin and making train travel attractive as a leisure activity for families. Borrowing from the success of Aer Lingus, female hostesses were introduced on main line routes from Dublin. Among the hostesses was a former insurance clerk, Margaret McGahern, whose recollections are entirely benign:

> I left insurance because women were not encouraged to regard it as a career, whereas I found being a hostess with CIÉ much more fulfilling. Although I have to say that it was very male—grandfathers to sons and on to their sons and so on . . . Going on business one day, the men were not sure if they should discuss railway business in front of me, until someone said, 'It's all right, Margaret is one of the boys.'
>
> The job meant the 'woman's work' of looking after children and invalids and old people. We were trained by a former chief air hostess. Families came to rely on us: young girls travelling on their own and that kind of thing. That early wave of tourist train-travellers of the 1960s were glad of us, because we had languages and

knew how to read maps and tourist sites and so on . . . It was a busy job, especially helping mothers with large families.

I remember a man and his wife emigrating. The man was being surrounded by his male friends, patting him on the back and saying how much they'd miss him. His wife was carrying the suitcases; she was trying to get in under the men's arms to get on the train. That's the kind of time it was . . .

Another picture—a young girl bringing a lovely baby up to Dublin for adoption. I noticed her because she was on her own and looked so sad. When I offered her company, we had a long chat on the journey—she was very clear about why she was giving up the baby. She was met at Kingsbridge by the social worker and I stayed with her for a while—everybody was being as kind as they could but the moment came and she handed it over in a waiting-room. Then she had to wait for the next train back and I had to go . . .

Then some months later I was helping a young couple with a new baby in a carrycot on the journey down south. The baby had red hair and so had the husband and I said it was easy to see where he got his colour from and they laughed. They had just taken it for adoption and were beside themselves with excitement. I offered to mind it while they went to the dining car. It was a very good baby and didn't cry. I don't think for a moment it was the same baby, but, you know, that was train travel.

I stayed five years and very fulfilling work it was.

Her time was during the seminal Andrews era, after which the system was in much better shape than when he took on the five-year mandate to 'cure or kill'. By March 1964 he had effected the Lemass mission, with closures of about one third of the system, a fall in the workforce of about 2,000 and a real reduction in costs, as defined by the Department of Finance. But baselines had also changed drastically in the prosperity of the early 1960s. Wages went up by about a third; the bus part of CIÉ's operations had damaging strikes and disruption. By the end of the period, in strict monetary terms, the state still needed to inject about £2m a year to balance the books and satisfy the Transport Act's requirement that 'expenditure should not exceed revenue'. In return, government was getting a slimmed-down, modernised rail network to meet the needs of an expanding economy in a rapidly changing country.

There was also a key change in the accounting methods by which the company's financial performance was judged. 'Grant-in-aid' replaced 'subsidy', 'subvention' and 'loss'—all terms which had negative resonances with politicians, the public and, crucially, senior civil servants—who were influential with transport ministers. Andrews brought about a sea change in awareness of the 'social service'

The way of the future

The new Enterprise, jointly operated by Iarnród Éireann and
Translink between Dublin and Belfast, at Balbriggan.

DART—Dublin Area Rapid
Transit—suburban service
between Bray, County Wicklow
and Howth, County Dublin,
pictured here at Killiney.

The modernised interior of
Heuston station.

value of the network and of the state's need to pay for it. Looking briefly ahead to the early 1980s and the ascent of the one-time clerk in Dromod station to the portfolio of Finance Minister, Albert Reynolds was to considerably extend that perception by funding the railways and the DART system.

Back in 1968, however, as Andrews relinquished his stewardship, the pared back system was closer to what it had been one hundred years before, in the heyday of railway making, operating the essential arterial routes, north, south, east and west. In the span of a century or so the railway age had peaked and settled. That enthusiasm of Pim, Dargan, MacNeill and thousands of railwaymen—fired by a dream—had settled down to a humdrum reality, from being the most revolutionary means of human mobility the island had seen.

Travel On . . .

There are as many books as there are railway routes. The following are recommended:

Doyle, Oliver, and Stephen Hirsch, *Railway in Ireland, 1834–1984*, Dublin: Signal Press 1983.

Murray, K. A., *Ireland's First Railway*, Dublin: Irish Railway Record Society 1981.

Murray, K. A., and D. B. McNeill, *The Great Southern & Western Railway*, Dublin: Irish Railway Record Society.

Ó Riain, Mícheál, *On the Move: Córas Iompair Éireann, 1945–95*, Dublin: Gill & Macmillan 1995.

Patterson, Edward, *The Great Northern Railways*, Oxford: Oakwood Press 1962.

Shepherd, Ernest, *Midland Great Western Railway: An Illustrated History*, Leicester: Midland Publishing 1994.

Specialist publications of:

Colourpoint Press, Gortrush, Omagh, County Tyrone

David & Charles, Newton Abbot, Devon

Midland Publishing, Leicester

Two works helpful to understanding the nineteenth century are *Railway Navvies* by Terry Coleman, London 1965, and *Letters from Ireland during the Famine of 1847* by Alexander Somerville, Dublin 1994. For the actual coaches, locomotives and inspiring memorabilia of the railway age, no source competes with the Ulster Folk and Transport Museum, Cultra, Holywood, County Down.

In Dublin, the collection of the IRRS at Heuston station will repay the forager for detail, as will the extensive records at the National Library. Local libraries, in particular Cork County Library, were extremely helpful. Apart from those credited in the text, many individuals were generous with their time and expertise, notably Oliver Doyle, Pat Hackett and Niall Torpey. Without the co-operation of the staff of Iarnród Éireann, neither this book nor the television series could have seen the 'light at the end of the tunnel'.